English Dialect Dictionary Online

Joseph Wright's *English Dialect Dictionary* (1898–1905) is the most comprehensive English dialect dictionary ever written, documenting in detail every dialect of English in the British Isles and Ireland, as well as the USA, Canada, South Africa and other colonial regions. Over the past ten years, it has been brought to life digitally as a freely available database resource, *EDD Online*, which provides access to this rich collection of dialect data. This book is a comprehensive user guide to *EDD Online,* showing how to get the most out of this unparalleled resource with step-by-step instructions, illustrated with handy screenshots, and an appendix containing full-colour figures. It also considers dialectological issues from phonetics to pragmatics and how searches can be tailored to specific linguistic concerns, demonstrating the interface's enormous potential to contribute to research in a range of disciplines, from dialectology to fields such as historical linguistics, corpus linguistics, lexicography and sociolinguistics.

MANFRED MARKUS is Professor Emeritus of English Linguistics at the University of Innsbruck and has published more than twenty books and two machine-readable corpora during his career. He has been director of the 'EDD Online' project since 2006.

English Dialect Dictionary Online

A New Departure in English Dialectology

Manfred Markus

University of Innsbruck

Shaftesbury Road, Cambridge CB2 8EA, United Kingdom

One Liberty Plaza, 20th Floor, New York, NY 10006, USA

477 Williamstown Road, Port Melbourne, VIC 3207, Australia

314–321, 3rd Floor, Plot 3, Splendor Forum, Jasola District Centre, New Delhi – 110025, India

103 Penang Road, #05–06/07, Visioncrest Commercial, Singapore 238467

Cambridge University Press is part of Cambridge University Press & Assessment, a department of the University of Cambridge.

We share the University's mission to contribute to society through the pursuit of education, learning and research at the highest international levels of excellence.

www.cambridge.org
Information on this title: www.cambridge.org/9781108814447

DOI: 10.1017/9781108886741

First published 2021
First paperback edition 2023

A catalogue record for this publication is available from the British Library

Library of Congress Cataloging-in-Publication data
Names: Markus, Manfred, author.
Title: English dialect dictionary online : a new departure in English dialectology / Manfred Markus.
Description: Cambridge, UK ; New York : Cambridge University Press, 2020. I Includes bibliographical references and index.
Identifiers: LCCN 2020036396 (print) I LCCN 2020036397 (ebook) I ISBN 9781108840651 (hardback) I ISBN 9781108814447 (paperback) I ISBN 9781108886741 (epub)
Subjects: LCSH: Wright, Joseph, 1855–1930. English dialect dictionary. I EDD online (Electronce resource) I English language–Dialects–Dictionaries.
Classification: LCC PE1766.W83 .M37 2020 (print) I LCC PE1766.W83 (ebook) I DDC 427.003–dc23
LC record available at https://lccn.loc.gov/2020036396
LC ebook record available at https://lccn.loc.gov/2020036397

ISBN   978-1-108-84065-1   Hardback
ISBN   978-1-108-81444-7   Paperback

Contents

Figures

Tables

Preface

This book is, first, intended for a general readership invited to share an unrivalled source of information on non-standard English dialects. Joseph Wright's *English Dialect Dictionary* (*EDD*; 1898–1905) is the most comprehensive of its kind ever published. Its newly available digitised version, *EDD Online (3.0)*, is a tremendous asset to our knowledge of English dialects if only for reasons of quantity. Yet the main strength of the online version is the unprecedented accessibility of dialect data due to *EDD Online's* elaborate interface.

This is where, second, professional academics as target readers can especially benefit. Many of the menus, parameters and filters explained and illustrated in this book will enable users to find answers to very specific questions about English dialects.

Given this dual target readership, this book aims to strike a balance in its descriptions of dialectological issues, keeping the technical explanations in Chapters 2–6 as simple and practical as possible, while discussing more challenging considerations in the second half of the book (Chapters 7–9). This bridging of the gap between dialect speakers/amateurs and dialect scholars is, in fact, in line with the legacy that Joseph Wright (1850–1930), both as a person and a scholar, left behind. Having grown up in a lower-class, poverty-stricken family, he was fascinated by studying the language of 'the people' in his later academic work.

My own encounter with the *EDD* and its remarkable compiler was essentially a coincidence. One day in 2002, while working in the reading room of the university library in Innsbruck, I came across a copy of Wright's *English Dialect Dictionary*. I had previously known of its existence, but I had never really used it. The six impressive volumes on the shelf awakened my immediate interest, as I had academically been involved in the historical varieties of English for a long time. On closer inspection, the idea started to grow in my mind that these comprehensive volumes had unfairly been neglected and ought to be digitised to be far more readily accessible. Earlier, I had studied some of the nineteenth-century dialect glossaries published by the *English Dialect*

Society. Having come across a large number of these glossaries in reprints stored in the library of the University of Augsburg, Germany, I had found them worth digitising.[1] But now I realised that Wright's *Dictionary* had incorporated many of those glossaries and was so much more substantial and, above all, systematic.

After this, it took some time until the first funded scholarly project on the *EDD* could be started, but at conferences, I frequently gave reports on the planned project and found that my concept fell on fertile ground with the international community of researchers in the field of corpus linguistics, though somewhat less so in the field of dialectology. The first *EDD* project, funded by the Austrian Science Fund (FWF), was carried out from 2006 to 2010, with Alexander Onysko as its manager and myself as director. But the money applied for had been reduced to a problematic minimum. Moreover, I was still burdened with the normal day-to-day academic work as my department's professor of linguistics and medieval English literature. No wonder that this project only created a beta version of the digitised *EDD*, not to be compared with *EDD Online 3.0*, but still most helpful in comparison to the paper version of the *EDD* and obviously used by quite a number of scholars and institutions ever since its publication – for example, by Oxford University Press in their work on the *OED*.

After retiring in 2009, I applied for a new project, *EDD Online*, which, after initial difficulties, once again turned out to be successful. The project was granted a period of up to five years and was accordingly run from April 2011 to March 2016. Since the money granted by the Austrian Science Fund (FWF) was again considerably less than what I had applied for, I decided to raise our working capacity by adding myself voluntarily, thus contributing twenty to thirty hours per week. In this way, I could also responsibly share daily decision-making.[2]

The project of 2011–2016 was, to be exact, a 'TR-project', which means a project pursuing aims and insights that can claim to be transferable in an interdisciplinary way to other fields of research. I trust that this claim has turned out to be justified. Some of the disciplines that may profit from *EDD Online* are dialectology, spoken language studies (orality), English historical linguistics (Late Modern English), lexicography and lexicology, corpus linguistics and computer philology.

Given that the second *EDD*-related Innsbruck project had not included the *Supplement* of the *EDD* and that, moreover, in its interface not all our dreams about an optimal query routine had come true, I applied for a second follow-up

---

[1] Cf. *English Dialect Society. Publications.* Nos. 1–80. 1873–1896. Kraus Reprint. An example of such reprints is Barnes (1886) (repr. Stevens-Cox 1970).
[2] The University of Innsbruck officially hired me for four hours per week.

project in 2016, which was granted and kept me and four team members busy for another eighteen months over 2017 and 2018, until October 2018. This third *EDD*-related project has not only enabled us to integrate the nearly 8,000 entries of the *Supplement* in our database but has also significantly enlarged and improved the potential of the interface, mainly in terms of correcting mistakes and quantifying query results. The details of what the *Supplement* has added will be discussed in their respective contexts below.

I am obliged to the Austrian Science Fund for the credit always given to my work and for having supported this project. My further thanks, being many, deserve acknowledgements in a section of their own.

Acknowledgements

Since *EDD Online 2.0* and *3.0* were follow-up projects, I am very much obliged to the work of the team of the previous Innsbruck project *SPEED* (*Spoken English in Early Dialects*: 2006–2010; *EDD Online 1.0*, for short), directed by myself and managed by Dr Alexander Onysko, supported by Dr Reinhard Heuberger, Mag. Christof Praxmarer, Mag. Christian Peer and the programmer Raphael Unterweger, who all did an excellent job. In hindsight, it is clear why the many problems involved could not all be solved. Now, with reference to *EDD Online 2.0* and *3.0* (2011–2018), it is more than routine for me, as both director and project manager, to express my thanks to all the collaborators of the first follow-up project for their help: Dr Emil Chamson, Stefan Giuliani and Christian Stenico as short-term members of the team, Daniela Jänsch, Anna-Maria Waldner and Regina Seiwald for their help over longer periods (more than a year). Mag. Andrea Krapf has been a team member over the project's full period of five years, and also in *EDD Online 3.0*. I am very much obliged to all of them, but particularly to Christian, Anna-Maria and Regina for their ever-industrious as well as intelligent and innovative cooperation. Andrea, as my 'right hand', has always been irreplaceable through the precision of her work and her sharp and critical mind. Whenever we tried to work out an optimal correction mode, improved our tagging system or wrote a new formula for XQuery, she was an ideally competent discussion partner, and in the final phase, she developed a particular expertise in creating complex XQuery formulas. Without her, the project would not have been finished in time.

Having participated in the daily routine myself, I cannot but sum up our teamwork with a feeling of deep contentment and gratitude. Somehow the project seems to have attracted only really good and pleasant juniors. In our practically daily tea and coffee breaks, we had wonderfully inspiring talks and I, as the senior member of the round, indulged in keeping in touch with what's going on in the minds of present-day 25- to 45-year-olds.

Raphael Unterweger of the DEA (Digitalisierung und elektronische Archivierung, University Library, Innsbruck), the programmer of our first project *SPEED* (Spoken English in Early Dialects; now *EDD Online 1.0*), has, in *EDD Online 2.0*, been occasionally available as an adviser whenever we needed him. At Trier (Germany), Dr Thomas Burch, of the Centre of Excellence at the university, accompanied our initial work as a most important first coach, also encouraging the corrective second typing of the whole Dictionary by a Chinese firm (thanks also to Dr Tao in Trier). Dr Hans-Werner Bartz, first in Trier and later at the German Academy in Mainz, supervised our work during the first two years of the project by regularly sending memos of mistakes and inconsistencies/bugs in our data. A great many thanks go to all these colleagues and helpers for supporting our work in its initial phase.

In the project's second phase, when we were in need of a programmer *in situ* and 'of our own', we happily found him in the person of Joachim Masser, who has been with us since summer 2013, accompanying our work with the XML-texts and initiating XPATH/XQUERY as our new database management. I am particularly obliged to Joachim for his cooperative working style, his benevolent attitude towards the project and his patience when confronted with philological issues. Roughly for the last year of the (second) project (April 2015 to March 2016), we fortunately hired – in addition to Joachim – a second programmer, who was mainly responsible for our web design. This was Martin Köll, who was, by his absolute professionality, alertness and competence, as well as by his friendliness and reliability, an enormous gain for the team. Thanks also go to Professor Emeritus Werner Wegstein of the University of Würzburg for his readiness to help in matters of TEI, the *Text Encoding Initiative*. Following his advice, we assimilated our tagging system to TEI, to align our XML-version to the now leading international standard.

I would also like to express my thanks to the administrative supporters of the University of Innsbruck, in particular, to Rector Professor Tilmann Märk, who allowed the project to have its necessary infrastructure, as well as to my wife, who often had to tolerate my absence from home at times (e.g. on weekends) when alluring mountains suggested 'something better to do'.

As regards the last (i.e. third) phase of the Innsbruck project work on the *EDD* (April 2017 to October 2018), my particular gratitude goes to Mag. Mirjam Hagen, our new team member, for her excellent work of tracing and correcting mistakes. She also kindly and competently helped me to format this book. Finally, I would like to express my thanks to my Innsbruck colleague Dr Leona Cordery, who has proofread the first draft.

Given my advanced age, I have managed to oblige three junior colleagues and friends to take care of *EDD Online (3.0)* in the future, particularly in view of the compatibility of our interface with browsers and the correction of major mistakes. The trio consists of my Innsbruck colleague Dr Reinhard Heuberger and my colleague at the University of Klagenfurt, Professor Alexander

Onysko, who were both involved in the earliest phase of the *EDD* projects, as well as Dr Joseph Wang, employee of the Innsbruck University institute of *Digital Humanities*, who will be of help locally in technical matters. I am very grateful to all of them for their readiness to stand in.

MANFRED MARKUS, *February 2019*

Note on the Text

Important note for online users: for the table of contents to pop up in the margin, please click on the blue icon for text markers (in the Adobe PDF-browser).

Users' comments on the *EDD Online* interface are always welcome and will be carefully considered. Please contact manfred.markus@uibk.ac.at

1 Introduction

1.1 Genesis of the *EDD*-Related Projects

EDD Online is a digitised version of Joseph Wright's *English Dialect Dictionary*, which was published from 1898 (or 1896[1]) to 1905 and covers the time from 1700 to 1904, with occasional, mainly etymologically motivated references to the preceding 1,000 years, that is, from 700 to 1700. The digitisation naturally implies OCR (optical character recognition). The paper version of the dictionary comprises some 4,600 pages, densely printed in two columns. The dialects depicted are those of the British Isles, historically including the whole of Ireland as well as the USA, Canada, Australia, South Africa and 'colonial' Englishes. The dictionary also includes what, from a later point of view, would be called 'sociolects', namely colloquial English, slang and cant, as well as 'technical' Englishes as used by professional groups such as farmers, miners and so on.

EDD Online is also the name of the last two Innsbruck *EDD*-related projects, supported by the *Austrian Science Fund* and aiming to provide an optimally digitised version of Wright's *Dictionary*. The first of the two projects lasted three years (1 April 2011 to 30 March 2014). The follow-up project, called *EDD Online: Applied, Corrected and Supplemented*, was carried out over eighteen months from 2017 to 2018. Both projects were based on the work of a previous project, *SPEED* (*Spoken English in Early Dialects*), which ran from 2006 to 2010 and had the purpose of presenting a preliminary online version of the *Dictionary*. The text of this initial phase was produced by a scanner and was not proofread, with the result of several unavoidable misreadings. The subsequent (automatic) tagging of the text was, naturally, insufficient, as was the interface provided for this data. But this first project was, in hindsight, an absolutely vital 'dress rehearsal' of our later performance.

---

[1] The earlier date is justified if one counts the pre-published fascicles, i.e. parts of the first volume. Part I – *A* to *Ballot* – was published on 1 July 1896 (cf. E. M. Wright 1932: II, 397). Volume I of the *EDD* in its complete form came out in 1898.

1

The two projects that have *EDD Online* in their names were, thus, the necessary follow-up projects of *SPEED*, with the aim of correcting the mistakes in *SPEED*, both of orthography and tagging. Moreover, the purpose of the follow-up projects was substantially to improve our interface, i.e. the surface on the screen allowing access to the *Dictionary*, in accordance with our corrections and with quite a number of better insights on what researchers can and will wish to do with Wright's *EDD*.

The official time of the second project was extended twice, each time for a year. The last project was planned for a year and a half from the very beginning. These extensions were unavoidable due to the enormous problems involved and despite our hard and keen work over the years. However, we did not require more money on our way, only more time. To put it in a simile close at hand in a town like Innsbruck, our work was like a mountaineering tour to an unknown peak, where one can never reliably predict when exactly one will reach it and when hard endeavour is finally rewarded by a fantastic view. Indeed, this is what *EDD Online*, after a long span of more than ten years of work on my part, finally offers: a fantastic view.

The changing names of the three *EDD*-related projects at issue here deserve a final remark. The names were mainly conditioned by the requirements of the Austrian Science Fund to which I gratefully owe the financial support. While the initial name, SPEED (for *Spoken English in Early Dialects*) was, in hindsight, an eye-catching misnomer, the last name has been too long to be worth remembering. So the two names may now be forsaken in favour of the names borrowed from the second phase of our project work so that we have the sequence *EDD Online 1.0*, *EDD Online 2.0* and *EDD Online 3.0*. Needless to say, when we now refer to *EDD Online* without adding the version, we, naturally, mean the output of the last of the three projects, *3.0*. A recent paper by Markus (2019a) has described the essential additions and innovations provided by version 3.0.

1.2   Overall Structure of the *EDD*

Apart from its paraphernalia (e.g. introduction, list of abbreviations, bibliography, *English Dialect Grammar*), the six volumes of the *EDD* (without the *Supplement*) that consist of some 64,500 entries are alphabetically arranged. To be more precise, the book comprises 71,484 headwords in 64,486 entries. The exactly 4,505 pages of the original dictionary do not include the *Supplement*, which is presented on pages 1–179 of volume VI because this contains, according to Wright, material 'the authority for which was not sufficient' (vol. VI, p. 1 of Suppl.). It also has a structure somewhat deviant from that of the main part of the *Dictionary*. We have, however, integrated Wright's list of *Corrigenda*, marking the necessary emendations in the XML-version of the running text by an attribute *sicCorr="true"*. Users finding passages in *EDD Online* that deviate from the original paper version of the *Dictionary* should, therefore, check the *Corrigenda* before they reclaim an error.

The later inclusion of the *Supplement* meant the addition of nearly 8,000 entries, which amount to about 11 per cent of the complete dictionary. The details of what the *Supplement* offers and in what way are described by Markus (2019b).[2] In a nutshell, the *Supplement* has added either new entries or new, in particular, semantic information on entries listed in the first place. Some entries are marked as questionable due to 'unsatisfactory authority', but the larger part of the entries simply provides new material.

All in all, the work of Wright and his team has turned out to be admirably scrupulous, knowledgeable and reliable. Nonetheless, it fairly soon became obvious in our correction work letter-wise that the *Dictionary* is not totally homogeneous in its use of descriptive features. Historical and etymological comments, as well as negative or somewhat half-hearted remarks, such as 'common in many parts of x', are considerably more frequent in letters *A* and *B* than in the other letters of the alphabet. Moreover, the *Dictionary's* complex syntax, i.e. the relationship of parts of entries to each other, turned out to be less consistent in the first few letters of the alphabet than with later ones, which suggests that Wright and his team were initially insecure in how to come to terms with the complexity of the data. Part of the 'learning process' on the part of the lexicographers seems to have been their elimination of an undue amount of phonetic or phonemic data (which we find on the first pages of the letter *A*) and to be more resolute concerning the in- or exclusion of material, whereas in *A*, there is still a striking number of comments and additions ranked to be of secondary relevance, mostly added in parentheses or brackets, with the result that these parts of the *Dictionary* are often structured less stringently than the others. Moreover, Wright, during his work on the *Dictionary*, seems to have changed his lexicographic method: from that of a nineteenth-century 'neo-grammarian' (in the way of, say, Alexander Ellis) towards that of a twentieth-century 'structuralist', with F. de Saussure *ante portas*.

Given all these factors of heterogeneity and inconsistency, we were initially (and occasionally) misguided by the first letters of the alphabet in coining tags which we later found to be rather irrelevant for the rest of the *Dictionary*. Another source of confusion was the inconsistent practice of abbreviating, in particular, concerning sources. A book reference to an author's name (like Bunyan), plus two words of the title, such as *Pilgrim's Progress*, may have been verbalised in up to ten different abbreviative versions. This, however,

---

[2] For a detailed discussion of the *Supplement*, see Markus (2019b).

came as no surprise, given that the *Dictionary* was compiled or prepared from the early 1890s up to 1905, i.e. for more than ten years, and that, naturally, typewriters (not to mention computers) were not available to handle the mass of data. All the more Wright's intuition in using abbreviative codes is to be admired, for example, in the reference to the main sources by way of indexed three-letter codes, such as 'Yks.13', where the numbers stand for titles 1 and 3 of the glossary books listed for Yorkshire in the bibliographical reference list.

1.3   Organisational

EDD Online (2.0) was started in the spring of 2011 when I had previously retired from my active work as a full professor of English linguistics and pre-1,500 literature at the University of Innsbruck. Given the situation in my department as it was, I decided to manage the new project myself, with practically daily presence in our project room in the University.

The project was funded by the Austrian Science Fund with the amount of €299,000, of which the University subtracted a lump sum of €50,000 for infrastructural costs. My team members and I accordingly obtained a project room and all the necessary equipment including computers and software from the University. We mainly used the XML-browser OXYGEN 14.1 and, later, 14.2, for which we got a licence from our computer centre. For programming we used, among other tools, XQuery, HTML, CSS (Cascading Style Sheets), JavaScript and Netbeans.

The follow-up project *EDD Online: Applied, Corrected and Supplemented* (i.e. *EDD Online 3.0*), running from April 2017 to October 2018, was a minor 'ORD project' of the Austrian Science Fund, the abbreviation *ORD* standing for an 'Open Research Data' pilot program,[3] with a budget of €61,000.

1.4   Survey of This Book

The purpose of this book is threefold. First, it familiarises readers with the diverse tools of *EDD Online* (3.0). Given the complexity of our interface (in line with the substance and structure of Wright's *EDD*), this 'handbook' part of the book by far outreaches the practical hints in the short *Guide* provided as part of the interface itself (cf. Markus 2017b). Second, by its going into depth on details of programming (though always from the linguist's and philologist's point of view), the present book wishes to address IT-specialists and laypeople working in philological projects of computerisation, in particular, in the digitisation of dictionaries. Describing the potential, but – in all frankness –

---

[3] This aims at latest technical standards in the digital age.

also the drawbacks and problems my team and I at the University of Innsbruck have been confronted with is meant to help other computer linguists solve their own problems if these are of a similar kind. With its occasional harping on technical detail, the book is also a documentation of the major part of our Innsbruck expertise as regards *EDD Online* – only after a year, many of these details will be only vaguely remembered or completely forgotten. Third, the book tries to have some impact on both English (computerised) lexicography and dialectology. While I strongly admire many of the outstanding achievements in the past of these two fields, I am also convinced that the new research tools now generally available can and should motivate us to practise new methods.

The method of this book is generally inductive rather than deductive. We will proceed from practical issues close at hand, such as those resulting from the orthography in the *EDD*, to more general topics concerning the use of *EDD Online*, the methods used for creating our data base and its dialectological and linguistic potential, with the overall line of thought more and more moving towards theoretical questions of dialectology and lexicography.

The book has, apart from the Preface, ten chapters. The first, introductory chapter familiarises the reader with the genesis of the Innsbruck project in its different phases and with the main aspects of the structure of the *EDD* as well as the organisational frame of our work in Innsbruck. It concludes with a survey of this book.

The subsequent three chapters (Chapters 2–4) proceed from the text's smaller units, such as the hyphen, special characters, issues of format and mistakes subject to emendation, to the important issue of tagging the original text in XML (Chapter 3) and the syntax of *EDD* entries in the face of the inherent hierarchy between their parts. The rules of TEI (the *Text Encoding Initiative*) are described as an answer to this hierarchical structure.

Chapter 5 mainly aims at corpus linguists and lexicographers as target groups, making practical suggestions based on our project work over the last fifteen odd years. The chapter provides some insights into the way we have digitised and tagged the text as well as a discussion of the software used for developing query commands. It will end with a flow chart purveying an idea of the division of labour practised in our Innsbruck project.

Chapter 6 throws light on the various functions of the *EDD Online* interface, proceeding from simple searches for headwords to the basic functional buttons and icons that are provided in and around the retrieval window (on the left of the interface screen) and then, in the way of a manual, discussing all the functions around the entry window (on the right of the interface screen). Since the icons for the filters are positioned there, 'around the entry window' means that the eight filters available in *EDD Online* are topicalised here in detail.

Chapter 7 returns to, and goes into depth on, the different sub-menus of the retrieval window (on the left of the interface), now with a focus on the 'advanced mode' parameters. By 'parameters' I here mean the types of text units that users can search for. They range from definitions and citations to compounds or other types of word formation and to phrases. Depending on which of the parameters has been opted for, the rules for the combination with other parameters and with filters vary.

Chapter 8 directs our attention to some exemplary research issues within English dialectology and language history to be encouraged by the search tools of *EDD Online*. The chapter first discusses the essence and *raison d'être* of (English) dialectology and then goes on to investigate, partly tentatively, some test cases offering themselves in the face of *EDD Online* as a new tool. A wide range of topics and tasks of dialectology are reflected in eight short studies, ranging from the 'UFO'-quality of dialectal variants to the ubiquity of Shakespeare in dialectal text and lexis. Given that the study of traditional dialects has never overcome its neo-grammatical nineteenth-century background, with its focus on individual words and the word forms of individual dialects, Chapter 8 may, hopefully, inspire dialectologists to try out new, more meaningful and less eclectic approaches.

One of the neglected aspects of traditional dialectology comes to bear in Chapter 9: quantification. The role of a dialectal form or meaning naturally depends very much on aspects of frequency. The counting of dialectal usage items is important in order for us to avoid unjustified generalisation and yet to come to terms with sub-systems of dialectal language. At the same time, measuring frequency presupposes clarity on what is being measured, and with what yardstick. Given that the *EDD* does not represent all counties and areas of the UK and of the English-speaking world alike and objectively, but with clear favourites, the chapter introduces and discusses the ways of normalising frequency figures, relating them to various sum totals. The visualisation of statistics on *ad-hoc* maps as they are provided in *EDD Online* is a further aspect of counting data with good reason and of interpreting them.

The final chapter (Chapter 10) provides, apart from an outlook, short information on the (general) availability of *EDD Online*. Readers of this book are strongly encouraged to test the interface and, thus, to fathom out the real potential of modern dialectology.

2   Orthography

2.1   General

We have tried to keep orthographic mistakes to a minimum by creating first a machine-scanned version of the whole text (in fact, the one used in the project *SPEED, alias EDD Online 1.0*) and then a double-typed version – typed by employees of a firm in China. The three versions were then automatically compared (by Hans-Werner Bartz of the University of Trier, later of the *Akademie der Wissenschaften* in Darmstadt, Germany), with a protocol listing the deviant passages so that we could check these passages and correct the mistakes manually. Generally, the mistakes made by the machine were different in type from the mistakes of the human typists. But talking about their mistakes, one should mention that the Chinese typists seemed to have a specific sense of deciphering subtle differences in graphic signs (which is what Chinese spelling consists of), in my opinion, more than educated European typists would, whose minds would probably have read and typed texts based on some sensible (but possibly incorrect) interpretation of words.[1] The *EDD*, of course, created specific problems of spelling semiotics: phonetic transcriptions (of a kind unknown today), with many special characters; pseudo-phonetic spellings (as were widely, but inconsistently common in nineteenth-century Britain); and, last but not least, problems caused by the wide use of abbreviations and the separation of words in line-, column- and page-breaks.

Unlike the main body of the *Dictionary*, the 179 pages of the *Supplement* were not produced in three versions, but only in a machine-scanned one, then to be manually corrected/proofread. This work filled part of the latest phase of the Innsbruck *EDD*-related project and in 2017, as before, was carried out within the XML-version of the text. The editor of OXYGEN 14 was again an

---

[1] This may be speculative reasoning, derogatory to Western typists, as one of my peer-group referees critically remarked. However, I had to take a decision on the optimal method of reproducing the text, and decisions are sometimes based on (prejudiced) experience.

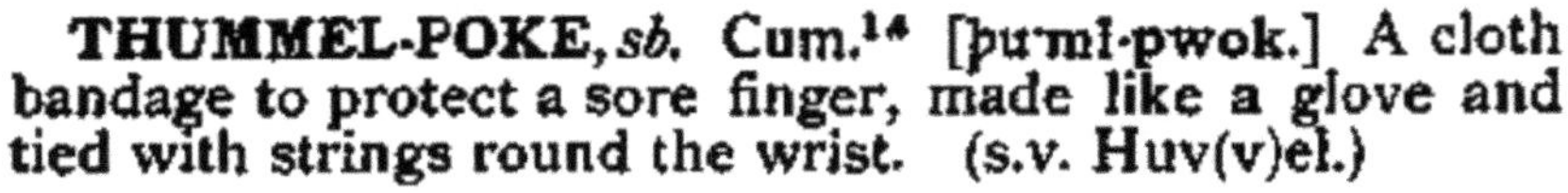

THUMMEL-POKE, *sb.* **Cum.**[14] **[þu·ml·pwok.] A cloth bandage to protect a sore finger, made like a glove and tied with strings round the wrist.   (s.v. Huv(v)el.)**

Figure 2.1 Use of the extra-short hyphen for compounds (example: THUMMEL-POKE)

appropriate tool for getting on with this task since many systematic scanning mistakes could be easily corrected globally.

2.2   The Problem of the Short Hyphen

Given that the *EDD* implies documentation of the use of mainly spoken English, the spelling of words was bound to be a problem, even to Wright himself. To give the first example: Wright generally used an extra-short hyphen for marking the elements of lemmatised compounds, as if he was uncertain about the value of these almost dot-like hyphens. See the headword in Figure 2.1.

Since dialect lexemes have always been mainly spoken words, Wright could not resolutely decide whether a compound such as *thummel(-)poke* was, or should be, hyphenated or not. The inconsistent use of the hyphen in the text citations, often added to illustrate the lemmas, reveals why Wright seemed unwilling to commit himself in the matter: separate spellings change with joined and clearly hyphenated spellings. In the face of this, Wright's extra-short hyphens in compounds occasionally seem intended as mere markers of morphemic boundaries. Unfortunately, there is no passage in the *EDD*'s editorial comments that explains this practice in further detail.

For a while we considered the possibility of keeping the extra-short hyphens, but then we anticipated the users' problems of interpreting them and, in queries, of typing the 'dubious dot' as a special character. We finally decided for just one type of hyphen, the normal one used today, in addition, of course, to the (somewhat longer) dash, which regularly stands for the substitution of a full word. The sign for the standard hyphen, thus, signals both a morpheme boundary and a possible hyphen proper.

2.3   Special Characters

Special characters were another general problem in reproducing the *EDD* on the computer. Using Unicode characters and, moreover, the coding system of TUSTEP (created at the University of Tübingen by Kuno Schälkle and Wilhelm Ott), we generated almost all the characters and diacritics we needed.

Only very rarely was a separation of diacritics from their graphs unavoidable, for example, initially for some short or long vowels, with both a hook and a stroke above them. But this problem was later solved by our programmers. We did, however, correct Wright's general merger of the *a*- and *o*-ligatures when italicised (<æ> misleadingly looking like <œ>), though this is a general problem that even present-day Microsoft WORD has left unsolved. We kept the two phonemes apart as best we could, based on phonological and etymological reasoning in each single case.

Another special problem we had to tackle was the merger of apostrophes and quotation marks in our initial scanning process. Wright has the two curbed single quotation marks for quotes (example: 'text'), sometimes with spaces before and after the text (' text '), and an equally curbed stroke for the apostrophe ('), which, on the pages of the book, often looks rather like a straight stroke ('). As could be expected, these signs were hopelessly mixed up. To have a clear distinction between the quotation marks and the apostrophe, we regularised the apostrophe to the single stroke ('), the more so since this sign is on the keyboard and does not need to be provided from a list of special characters.

In various other cases, special characters could not be avoided. Thus the ampersand sign '&' had to be coded (&), just like the protected space between parts of headwords ( ) and various phonemic or phonetic symbols with ligatures, accent or stroke superscripts, to mention only these few cases.

2.4   Format

In the *EDD* entries, there are extra-wide spaces (so-called 'spatia') for keeping certain sections of the entries apart. The difference to normal spaces is, however, so minimal that both our scanner and the Chinese typists failed to reproduce them. We did not see sufficient reason for manually reproducing this specificity of format, unlike various other format items (such as boldface), for two reasons (apart from the difficulty of tracing the spatia). (a) In our XML-version of the text (XML = 'Extended Markup Language') each single word has all the functional attributes ('tags') it needs for the researcher's retrieval – see Chapters 3 and 4. All the *prima-facie* formatting of the *EDD* in book form, including font size, types of fonts, small capitals and so on, are, therefore, redundant text features and were seen by us as secondary. (b) The user of *EDD Online* can always switch to the original image of an entry to check what a specific passage or word in the entry looks like. This option of the possible investigation of the original meant a large amount of extra work for us: each word in each line had to be given its specific coordinates in terms of the four corner points of the image. But we have always wished our output to be subject to users' immediate control. With all this particular care taken by us to allow reproducing the original entry and, moreover, a special string in an entry, we invite all users to inform us about mistakes, should any still be found, or inconsistencies in our text in relation to the original image.

2.5   Emendations

Only very rarely did we have to correct what we found in black and white in the *Dictionary*. Emendation proper has been applied in cases of clear misprints, for example in the case of *brist e-fern*, where an obviously missing <l> (*bristle-fern*) has not come out in the printing (in the entry MAIDEN). We did not comment on such cases, which can be easily interpreted in their contexts, but silently emended these rare passages, not without leaving traces in the XML-version of the text by adding the attribute *sicCorr="true"*. Of course, attributes are not visible to the users in our interface, but can only be checked in the XML-text, which we will keep under strict custody.[2]

Moreover, where there have been inconsistencies in the entries, for example, in the counting of items (e.g. when there was a (2), but no (1)), we have likewise emended the mistakes because they would have irritated the computer's query routines. Such corrections have also always been marked by the attribute *sicCorr="true"*. The same holds true for (rare) emendations caused by 'retrieval deficits'. For example, when the *EDD* referred to a numbered compound as part of, and only used within, a phrase, we had to mark both the compound and the phrase with the given *numerus currens* for the computer to find the quotations and sources attributed to the compound in the subsequent paragraph of the text.[3] The number of the compound was, therefore, repeated by us before the phrase and marked, as all insertions, by double curly brackets to signal the emendation. The interface screen, by the way, presents such emendations by their grey, rather than black, colour.

In addition to these emendations, we had to think of the mistakes corrected by Wright himself. He added half a page of *Corrigenda* at the end of his *Dictionary*, after the *Supplement* (vol. 6, page 179). We have integrated all

---

[2] This is only meant to exclude non-transparent competitive modifications of our interface. Further enhancement of the work done in Innsbruck in the form of joint ventures would, of course, be welcome.

[3] For example, a compound x listed under (14) in an entry is only attested as part of phrase xy. The quotation and/or source added in the subsequent paragraph under (14) would only be found by the computer in relation to compound (14), but not in relation to the phrase as part of which the compound has survived. The quotation and its source, however, apply to the phrase as much as to the compound.

these corrections in the XML-version of the text and marked them there by an attribute *ana="sicCorr"*.[4]

2.6   Summary

The use of deviant special characters and diacritics in historical texts, trivial to say, can be quite a nuisance. The problems involved have pursued us to the very end of the project. They began with the often illegible quality of deviant characters (also deviant in format, e.g. by being italics), where illegibility mostly means misinterpretation by the scanner. Afterwards, when the 4,650 pages of text were 'in the box', the challenge continued when all kinds of small programs, for example, written for sorting lists of retrievals in different ways, had to take notice of the special role of certain characters and signs. Parentheses, numbers and diacritics are apt to disturb alphabetical orders and have to be specially defined. Finally, there have been many signs, such as the curly brackets for emendations, which we had to define as relevant in queries, but they were meant to disappear on the interface page.

The structure of our XML-text, with one line reserved for each single word of the original (see Chapter 3), was a good strategy for the correlation of the text with the images of the *EDD* book version behind the text. The initial correction work was also easier to achieve with isolated lexemic units at our disposal. However, many strings isolated in the original – by a hyphen, by a line- or paragraph break or simply by a space (as in the case of many English compounds and compositions) – later had to be joined together to be accessible by the computer.

The general word orientation of a dictionary and of our XML-text was also thwarted by Wright's 'intuitive' concept of what a word is. The *headwords* range from single phonemes and morphemes to complete phrases so that the definition of a lexeme by its orthographic appearance proved impossible, at least theoretically. In practical terms, the evidence of inconsistency in Wright's policy of lemmatisation is exceptionally striking at the beginning of the *Dictionary*, in the letter *A*. By and large and from a human point of view, the *Dictionary* is remarkably consistent and admirably thorough, not the least in its fastidious orthography.

---

[4] The names of attributes, such as 'ana' (for 'analysis'), were, as the names of our tags, strongly conditioned by the rules of TEI, to be discussed in Section 4.2.

3 Tagging

3.1 Survey

In the XML-version of the text, every word in the *Dictionary* is related by identity numbers to one particular entry and to a particular line, column and page. Moreover, each string is marked by its 'role' in the text via a 'tag': headword, part of speech (e.g. verb), dialect area identified by county, and so on. To keep the tagged text relatively short, we have abbreviated most of the tags, for example, *pos* for 'part of speech' and, in line with Wright, *Yks.* for 'Yorkshire' as the county where the string or word at issue was used.

Most words/strings have a linked combination of tags whenever they belong to different groups. Thus, a *pos*-marker may be part of the formal equipment of, for example, a headword concerned. The hierarchical relationship between tags is signalled by the combination with a subscript minus sign, as in the tag-group *form_pos*, which usually follows the tag *form_orth* (for 'orthography'). The example shows that some of the tags, in this case *form*, are constructed as common denominators/cover terms or 'parents'. In general, there are several levels of hierarchy (up to, or even beyond, ten), for example, in the tag *form_variant_title_biblio*, where *form* stands for the formal and initial part of the entries and marks the direct relationship to the headword, *variant* for (mostly) spelling variants of the headword, *title* for the source(s) attributed to that particular variant (again a parent construct), and *biblio* for a particular subtype of sources, namely those on dialects.

In our tagging work, it soon turned out that 'biblio', like many other tags, was not a 'decent' tag in the world of TEI, the *Text Encoding Initiative*, so that we had to replace it. This addresses a specific problem to be dealt in Section 3.2.

The *EDD* entries ideally consist of six main sections, giving rise to six main tags, namely: (1) *form*; (2) *sense*; (3) usage (*usg*); (4) *re* (*re*ference to entry), that is the cover-tag for derivations, compounds, so-called combinations, and phrases; (5) *cit* (*cit*ations, for quotations from sources); and (6) *comment* (for bracketed additions of a usually lower degree of relevance). As the survey shows, the formal and semantic description of a dialect word (see points (1) and (2)) is by no means sufficient. In fact, the features grouped in (3)–(6) are the more challenging ones. *Usage* (*usg*), for example, is concerned with, as it were, the wh-questions to be raised on dialect words, the when, where and how of their occurrence. *Usg*, accordingly, branches into *date*, *area (county/region/ nation)* and *label*, to mention only these three for the time being. By the same token, the other main tags (4)–(6) branch into further 'children'. *Re*, for example, is a parent tag for various types of word composition mentioned earlier, such as compounds. When we focus on a particular compound within an entry, there are a number of details that describe this compound. Our tagging system here turns out to be recursive, with all the tags on the first sub-level of an entry applying again in that the compound has (or may have) features of form, sense, usage-related information, citations and comment notes.

Our programmed query routine had to be prepared for any feature that may occur, even if only once. In concrete entries of the *EDD*, however, not all tags theoretically possible on the different levels are always needed. To demonstrate what the 'average' entry, with its specific features, looks like I select a relatively simple example.

3.2   The Tags in Context

The six main tags just mentioned play a non-correlative role in the layout of the entries: there are not six, but basically four paragraphs containing the six tags (= functions). This is illustrated in Figure 3.1.

AFTER-DAMP, *sb.* Tech. Nhb. Dur. w.Yks. [aˑ**ftə-damp**.]
The noxious gas resulting from a colliery explosion
(Wedgwood).
Nhb. & Dur. After-damp, carbonic acid, stythe. The products
of the combustion of fire-damp, NICHOLSON *Coal Tr. Gl.* (1888)
Nhb.1 After-damp, the noxious gas resulting from a colliery explosion.
This after-damp is called choak-damp and surfeit by the
colliers, and is the carbonic acid gas of chymists, HODGSON *A
Description of Felling Colliery.* **w.Yks.** The after-damp completed
their death, *N. & Q.* (1876) 5th S. v. 325. Miners' tech. Carbonic
acid gas, or choke damp, which the miners call after-damp, Core
(1886) 228.
[*After + damp*, q.v.; cp. **choak-damp**.]

Figure 3.1 Main tags and layout in *EDD Online* (example AFTER-DAMP)

The four main parts/paragraphs of the entry AFTER-DAMP can be identified as follows:

(1) First line (= 'head'): information on formal aspects of the lemma, i.e. its orthography (in our tagging system: *form_orth*, with the searchword AFTER-DAMP highlighted in yellow), its part of speech (*form_pos*) in red, a usage label (in this case a pragmatic one, labelprag [*Tech*]), a list of areas, in this case counties, with Yorkshire specified by the direction *w.*, all in brown, and, finally, the phonetic transcription (tagged by us as *form_pron*). The abbreviations for the dialectal areas stand for Northumberland, Durham and West Yorkshire.
(2) The second and third lines, that is, the second (short) paragraph: here, semantic information on the lemma (*sense*) is provided. The line contains a definition of the headword, plus the name of the authority, that is, the sources which this definition is based on.
(3) The paragraph of citations or quotations: this paragraph, written in a smaller font than the previous text, presents evidence by citations from sources, with these and their dates of publication and further details (exact pages, etc.) added.
(4) A comment attached in some of the entries at their end: comments contain information of somewhat secondary relevance, that is, information which does not directly refer to dialect attribution but to language history, etymology, or word formation, and often also includes cross-references.

The subordination of the first five sub-tags to the form of the 'head' has been necessary to mark their correct reference, thus keeping them apart from the more specific attribution to dialect areas in the block of citations, for example, to Nhb. right at the beginning of that block. This is a first example of the fact that the layout structure of the entries (paragraphs) does not completely map their functional units. Accordingly, in addition to the four main tags, we had to implement seven further major ones in the course of our work. On the one hand, special types of word formation or word collocation play quite an important role in Wright's *Dictionary*, namely derivations (*deriv*[1]), compounds (*comp*), combinations (*comb*) and phrases (*phr*). On the other hand, grammatical forms, such as *prp.* (for 'present participle'), and variants of dialect words are so often listed in detail and so important in the dialect attribution that we have defined them as autonomous categories of tags. Moreover, we had to add the tag *mix* for lists of different types of word formation so that the complete number of main tags came to fifteen (Figure 3.2).

On average, each of these fifteen tags turned out to dominate some twenty sub-tags so that the sum total of all the tags amounted to about 300. This complexity is due to Wright's keen philological approach, providing information on various aspects of language, including some which had not been named linguistically in his days. This holds particularly true for word formation and pragmatics. As mentioned earlier, the *EDD* entries often include composite words and phrases. The derivations are usually introduced by

---

[1] This and the following abbreviations are always the tag used by us for the given item.

1. form/head	orthography (1)	
		part of speech (pos) (2)
		usage label (3)
		area of dialect (4)
		phonetic (5)
2. sense	meaning proper (6)	
		derivations (7)
		compounds (8)
		combinations (9)
		phrases (10)
		mix (11) (a mixture of 7-10)
		grammar (12)
		variant (13)
3. citation	citation (14)	
4. comment	comment (15)	

Figure 3.2 Survey of main tags (in our original tag terminology)

'Hence', the compounds by the introductory formula 'Also in comp.', and so on with phrases and so-called combinations. 'Combinations' are mostly two-word compositions with separate spelling. Onysko (2010: 143) showed that they are typologically fuzzy, overlapping, to some extent, with both compounds and phrases.[2] Pragmatics, for its part, plays a major role in many of the *EDD*'s usage labels, not surprisingly since the *EDD,* as a whole, often includes behavioural and cultural aspects of dialect use (cf. Heuberger 2010). Accordingly, quite a number of words or phrases are marked by a reference to the typical speaker or addressee involved. We have tried to find such references by tracing expressions such as 'used by' (e.g. applied to children) or 'used to' (e.g. 'used to address horses').

3.3   How the Tags Were Created

In general, the tagging, after its very basic automatic initial phase, had to be carried out manually or semi-manually. This was performed in the original XML-texts using the browser OXYGEN 14.2. To provide an illustration of just one line of the *EDD* in XML, here is the first line of the entry LAAG, exceptionally presented in a condensed and small font to avoid line breaks (Figure 3.3).

As Figure 3.3 shows, XML allows for each word of the *Dictionary* to have a line of its own so that the text proper has to be read vertically. The line is opened before the text starts (<line ...>) and then closed at the end of the text (</line>). The strings of the original text are now the 'values' of 'elements', that is, of 'tags', which are presented at the beginning of every line. The rest of the lines, that is, their greater part, is used for 'attributes' of the elements,

---

[2] Onysko hypothetically suggests that Wright used the broad category of 'combination' where there were 'no clear indications about the degree of lexicalisation of these units in the respective dialects' (143).

```
<line newid="LL00026" b="2211" baseline="2202" id="L26" l="298" r="1493" t="2155">
<Head_word value="LAAG," newid="W01" b="2209" fontSize="10.0" id="W241" l="298" r="459" t="2166" />
<head_pos value="v.2" newid="W02" b="2200" fontSize="10.0" id="W242" italic="true" l="479" r="532" t="2163" />
    <head_county value="Sh.I." newid="W03" b="2199" fontSize="10.0" id="W243" l="579" r="679" t="2162" />
    <phono value="[låg.]" newid="W04" b="2208" fontSize="10.0" id="W244" l="731" r="842" t="2161" />
    <meaning value="To" newid="W05" b="2196" fontSize="10.0" id="W245" l="889" r="946" t="2160" />
    <meaning value="pour" newid="W06" b="2205" fontSize="10.0" id="W246" l="972" r="1072" t="2170" />
    <meaning value="water" newid="W07" b="2194" fontSize="10.0" id="W247" l="1095" r="1215" t="2164" />
    <meaning value="on" newid="W08" b="2194" fontSize="10.0" id="W248" l="1240" r="1289" t="2170" />
    <mn_fct value=";" newid="W09" b="2202" fontSize="10.0" id="W249" l="1307" r="1316" t="2171" />
    <meaning value="to" newid="W10" b="2194" fontSize="10.0" id="W250" l="1342" r="1380" t="2163" />
    <meaning value="bale" newid="W11" b="2193" fontSize="10.0" id="W251" l="1405" r="1493" t="2155" />
</line>
```

Figure 3.3 XML-text (with the tags originally used)

among these a new ID number ("newid"), which we entry-specifically added to the original ID number.[3]

Such information may be of little interest to some readers. Indeed, there is no need to explain the details of the XML-text and of the excellent possibilities of OXYGEN 14.2 as regards find–replace routines, filtering possibilities and the definition of variables. All in all, the correction of the tags (plus that of the attributes, to be discussed in Section 5.4) cost us more than a year of correction work (of at least three part-time team members). Suffice it to say here that the tags are not only of interest individually but also as clusters. For example, variants are tagged consistently as 'variant', no matter which main block or cover-tag they belong to so that *form_variant, sense_variant* (in the block of definitions), *deriv_variant, comp_variant,* and so on can be retrieved either as part of their respective groups or irrespective of these groups. The same principle applies to the additional descriptive features of variants, for example, concerning their dialect areas (e.g. *comp_variant_county*).

3.4   Special Problems with Tags: The Separate Numbering

One of the specific difficulties we encountered, however, is worth mentioning. It was caused by Wright's practice of numbering the listed meanings, citations, compounds, variants, and so on, with the effect that there is an implicit correlation between the meanings, enumerated by *numerus currens*, and the citations in the subsequent paragraphs illustrating these meanings. We therefore had to tag the numbering system as well, with up to five hierarchical levels of counting. There were entries with numerical sequences of well over 100, in entries that reach a length of ten pages or more.

---

[3] This original ID-number, which we later gave up, was rigorously sequential throughout the whole *Dictionary* and, thus, brought us very high figures.

The tags and sub-tags were coined in answer to the complex structure of Wright's *Dictionary*, with information not just on the existence of dialect words and their local attribution, but on all kinds of linguistic aspects including pragmatics, morphology and prosody, as well as historical features such as etymology. In our project, we aimed to mark pieces of information in the *Dictionary* in an optimal way from a modern linguistic standpoint. It would, however, be premature now to illustrate this practice of tagging and to concern the reader with its snags. Most users of *EDD Online* will probably be more interested in the interface (the query mask) and its possibilities of retrieval, and the discussion of our interface in Chapter 5 will indirectly reveal the amazing complexity of the *EDD* as grasped by our tags.

Yet, it should be emphasised that scrupulous tagging is important because the interface can, naturally, only retrieve items that have been appropriately tagged. In our case, a large number of manual tagging corrections were necessary, as, due to the unpredictability of many items, global marking only functioned up to a point. For users interested in the method of our tagging, Chapter 4 discusses the details.

4 The Syntax of *EDD* Entries, and How to Describe It

4.1 The Potential and Limitation of Our Initial Tags

When we started tagging, we aimed to grasp as many features of the entries as seemed sensible from a philological point of view. However, we met with many difficulties. For example, the 74,000 odd entries included many word-like subsections on compounds, derivations and phrases, most of which would be lemmatised in modern dictionaries. This double membership of such types of word formation as both (formal) 'sub-lexemes' and (functional) lexemes in their own rights naturally increased the difficulty of consistently describing the structure of the *Dictionary*. As regards the dialect distribution of words or forms, Wright has provided information on three different levels: counties (such as Yorkshire), regions (such as East Anglia) and nations, such as England, Scotland, Wales and so on. As to sources, the *EDD* distinguishes special literature on dialects (which we have finally tagged as title_BIBLIO[1]) from literary texts (such as poems or fiction, which we have called title_LIT).[2] A further source category is that of unprinted information attributed by correspondents (which we have tagged as title_CORRESP). In the case of usage labels, which the *EDD* provides in abundance, we coined eight basic sub-types, from frequency (LABELFREQ) and reliability (LABELREL) to sub-labels concerning phonology, prosody, morphology, syntax, semantics and pragmatics. Dialect areas and usage labels are unquestionably the two most relevant search filters. The remaining six, for which all strings concerned had to be identified by (capitalised) attribute tags, are *parts of speech, phonetic, etymology, morphemic* and *time spans*.

---

[1] 'Finally' refers to the TEI-conditioned mode we implemented fairly late in the course of the project. The capitalisation of tags means that they turned out to be unacceptable in the TEI syntax as proper tags (i.e. elements) and had to be automatically changed later to have the status of 'attributes'.

[2] Dialect authors have been inconsistently attributed by Wright to either 'general dialect literature' or 'literature'. In our interface, we have tried to keep the two groups apart up to a point, with dialect fiction generally included in 'literature'. However, given the large amount of sources and the difficulty of separating the two types reliably, our interface provides a third option of sources that includes both types.

<dictScrap_CIT_span_NUM value="(66" n="W03394"
  facs="t=578,b=618,l=633,r=690" rendition="startSource" />

<dictScrap_CIT_title_BIBLIO_district_PREC_span_XNUM value="a" n="W03395"
  facs="t=589,b=617,l=711,r=745" />

<dictScrap_CIT_title_BIBLIO_district_PREC_span_XNUM_ex value=","
  n="W03396" ana="pc_prae" />

<dictScrap_CIT_title_BIBLIO_district_PREC_span_XNUM value="b)" n="W03397"
  facs="t=578,b=619,l=761,r=793" rend="italic" />

<dictScrap_CIT_title_BIBLIO_district_PREC value="n.Yks.2" n="W03398"
  facs="t=579,b=610,l=810,r=948" />

<dictScrap_CIT_district_PREC_span_XNUM value="(c)" n="W03399"
  facs="t=578,b=620,l=993,r=1037" rend="italic" />

<dictScrap_CIT_district_PREC value="e.Yks." n="W03400"
  facs="t=582,b=610,l=1061,r=1178" style="abbr" />

<dictScrap_CIT_title_BIBLIO value="Nicholson" n="W03401"
  facs="t=578,b=608,l=1196,r=1400" />

<dictScrap_CIT_title_BIBLIO value="Flk-Sp." n="W03402"
  facs="t=575,b=616,l=1415,r=1551" rend="italic" style="abbr" />

<lb n="W03403" facs="t=617,b=662,l=322,r=1553" />

<dictScrap_CIT_date_PUBL_pc value="(" n="W03404" ana="pc_post" />

<dictScrap_CIT_date_PUBL_term value="1889" n="W03405"
  facs="t=617,b=658,l=322,r=437" />

<dictScrap_CIT_date_PUBL_pc value=")" n="W03406" ana="pc_prae" />

<dictScrap_CIT_date_PUBL_surplus value="4" n="W03407"
  facs="t=629,b=657,l=454,r=473" ana="s_prae" />

<dictScrap_CIT_date_PUBL_pc value=";" n="W03408"
  facs="t=630,b=657,l=487,r=495" ana="pc_prae" />

Figure 4.1 Average tag concatenation, in bold (random example)

However, the *Dictionary*'s wealth of information is not only based on the high number of element tags and attributes but also on the diverse relationships between them due to the complex syntax of the entries. The relationship may be more or less hierarchical: LABELFREQ, for example, may define the (frequent or less frequent) usage of a phrase, which may be part of a word's 'definition', which, for its part, may be attributable to a specific meaning of a compound, which may be listed as number (3) of the headword's different meanings ('senses') and is correlated to number (3) in the subsequent paragraph providing evidence in citations/quotations. In the *EDD*, we have hierarchies of up to ten levels. They have found their expression in the number of concatenated tags, as shown in Figure 4.1.

The little bit of original text depicted by the elements and attributes of Figure 4.1 is as follows:

(66, a, b) n.Yks. Nicholson Flk-Sp.
  (1889) 4;

Trying to describe such relationships as precisely as possible, we followed the advice initially given by our partners at the Excellence Centre of the University of Trier, using a 'vertical' system of XML-text presentation. This allows one line for each single word/string. It was, thus, possible to attribute all the features necessary to mark every single text unit. As Figure 4.1 shows, each line carries a piece of information under the attribute name 'facs', which stands for 'facsimile' and was automatically produced in the original scanning process. The first line, for example, has *facs="t=578,b=618,l=633,r=690"*. The four letters and numbers identify the word's coordinates on the original page of the *EDD* (top/bottom/left/right). Using these coordinates, the words concerned can be identified by our interface in the image of an entry or, rather, on the page of that entry.

The tags we initially coined were short, suggestive of what they stand for, and as consistent as they could be. We were, however, then strongly advised to adopt the now leading international tagging norm of historical texts called Text Encoding Initiative (TEI). The extra work caused by the transfer to this coding system was enormous.

4.2   The Challenge of TEI

TEI is an elaborated network of tags and attributes. While the dictionaries, philological texts and manuscripts for which these tags of elements and attributes were originally made seem to be different in structure from 'our' dictionary, we tried – for nearly half a year – to adapt our element tags and attributes to the version of TEI available at the time (2013), the reason being that the *EDD* should not be internationally isolated when finished. From my point of view, the main weakness of the TEI codes for elements is that they scrupulously focus on rather traditional manifestations of form, particularly the form of old manuscripts, but have generally ignored or neglected modern linguistic issues such as word formation, semantics, pragmatics, and what English lexicographers call labels and variants. As regards word formation, for example, the *EDD*'s different types of lexemes (derivations, compounds, phrases, and Wright, moreover, uses 'combinations' as another category) – all these subtypes of lexemes had to be re-tagged by us along the lines of TEI, partly by using circumscriptive tag-clusters so that we ended up with, for example, an artificial 're', standing for 'reference', as a cover-tag, with the essential feature 'compound', or whichever other type of word formation was at issue, relegated to the inferior position of an 'attribute'; we marked this position by capitalisation. Similarly, we had to use somewhat non-suggestive tags such as 'dictScrap' or 'note' as cover-tags for important parts of the *Dictionary*, such as citations and the different types of labels. As a result of this necessary rewriting procedure, many features that we had considered to be important were not grasped as element tags, as they should have been, but by 'attributes'.[3] In this way, our tagging system became less and less self-evident and lost its former transparency.

Despite such often frustrating 'detours' in our tagging, we are still glad to have implemented TEI, triggered by our cooperators at the University of Trier (Centre of Excellence: Dr Thomas Burch, Dr Hans-Werner Bartz) and also by Professor Emeritus Werner Wegstein, University of Würzburg. Apart from its internationality, TEI has caused us to reconsider the logic of our tags as to hierarchy. What does a particular piece of information exactly refer to? What is the range of a certain piece of information? Which parameters had rightly been defined as element tags and which were more sensibly or necessarily attributes?

The exact understanding of the complex 'syntax' of the entries in the *EDD* is something our team could already boast of only after months of keen endeavour. I myself have preliminarily investigated this complexity of the entries in previous papers, for example, in Markus (2012). Suffice it to illustrate the point here with an example. The value of the abbreviation 'Yks.' (for 'Yorkshire') has to be interpreted in its context, which raises two questions: (1) what does the information refer to? and (2) is the string 'Yks.' somehow specified?

As regards the first question, of reference, the given information of dialect attribution may refer to a lemma as a whole, or to a spelling variant of it, or to its pronunciation, or to a compound that contains the lemma string, or a combination or derivation or phrase of the same type, or to a quotation that illustrates the use of any of these forms just listed. Or, to finish the list, the reference to 'Yks.' may be part of an entry-final comment. A major problem with the quotations was that they frequently do not immediately follow their referents, that is, the units they are meant to illustrate, but at a distance. As mentioned earlier, the reason for this is that the *EDD* usually lists, for example, compounds formed with the lemma term in a numbered order, coming back to these numbers in the subsequent paragraph, where the compounds previously listed are illustrated in quotes. The rules dominating such *post festum* information were not easy to analyse, the more so since there are various

---

[3] The rule of thumb for the difference between element tags and attributes is that primary features should be grasped by the former, whereas features of secondary importance by the latter. 'Importance' here means the role of features in the query routine.

hierarchical counting systems involved in the *EDD*, from I./II./III. and 1./2./3. via (1)/(2)/(3) to (a)/(b)/(c) and even (α)/(β)/(γ).

The second problem we faced was the frequent specification of the dialect marker. Trying to testify to a form's occurrence in Yorkshire dialect (as an example), we had to make sure that the string 'Yks.' was not part of some longer string such as 'e. Yks.' or 'sw. Yks.', or of phrases such as 'in some southern parts of Yks.'. To keep such different types of 'hits' separate, we created four categories (expressed by attributes): PREC (for exactly Yorkshire), DIRECTION (for East/South etc. Yorkshire), PART (for cities/rivers in Yorkshire) and FUZZY (for more or less vague statements of the type 'in some parts of Yorkshire'). These four categories are provided in our interface to be activated in optional combination. The default mode, however, is that all four attributes are switched on.

In addition to these four types of referential precision, we had to interpret Wright's abbreviative practice: 'Yks.123' is a reference to three books listed as Yks.1, Yks.2 and Yks.3 in the *EDD* bibliography and at the same time implies that the item at issue is affiliated with the county of Yorkshire in that the sources of the given quotations testify to language use there. This referential complexity did not exactly make our programming work easier. The compatibility restrictions imposed by TEI, while necessary in principle, meant an extra barrier for our work because linguistically descriptive texts, not to mention dictionary texts, are obviously not the kind of text the originators of TEI initially had in mind. The TEI guidelines are permanently being revised. Hopefully, one of the next revisions takes the working terms of modern and historical linguistics into account more decidedly than has been the case so far.

4.3   Conclusion

Much more could be said about XML and TEI, for example, that the former implies a linear encoding of a text, the latter a hierarchical one. A glimpse into arithmetics may be helpful to illustrate the difference for IT laymen. The simple sequence (a+b) × c+d is different from (a+b) × (c+d). Like the first formula, XML does not care about hierarchy, but it is based on a strictly linear order, whereas TEI is mainly concerned with hierarchy. However, being a philologist myself, I can, in hindsight, only say that such corpus-linguistic tools can less easily be acquired theoretically than in line with the principle of learning by doing. In Chapter 5, we therefore return to concrete issues concerning the creation of *EDD Online*, listing some suggestions for future work with complex text structures and, in particular, historical dictionaries.

5   Some Practical Suggestions in Hindsight

5.1   The Text

The initial production of a double- or triple-text version, with one text created by a scanner and optical character recognition (OCR), the other (or rather two of them) by human (in our case, Chinese) typists, still seems to me to have been the optimal mode for the reliable digital reproduction of the text. The achievement of the Chinese typists was admirable. The automatic comparison of the human versions with our machine version, in the form of a 'protocol' of deviations, was a good foundation for our subsequent manual correction. Normal 'manual' proofreading of a text such as Wright's *EDD*, the mode suggested in one of our earlier external expert reports, would have been practically impossible, given the small size of the fonts, the often confusing layout, the disconcerting and erratic spellings of dialect texts and the length of the *Dictionary*. We used this homemade mode of proofreading for the 179 pages of the *Supplement*, later added to the dictionary proper. In my view, our negative experience then confirmed the earlier assumption that Western readers/typists (rather than Chinese ones, with their strong sense of formal detail) may not have been able to do the job as satisfactorily. The text extract of Figure 5.1, from the entry of the verb and noun *GO*, may serve to illustrate this point of the *EDD*'s relative inaccessibility to typists.

Apart from the correct deciphering of 'normal' strings by the computer, the competent interpretation of diacritical signs in the text, as well as hyphens, quotation marks, apostrophes and other marks of punctuation (or signs in the phonetic transcription), was part of the important step of providing a solid text foundation. Admittedly, we initially underestimated the implications of this point. For example, full stops and parentheses were either part of a string, as in the case of enumerations, for example, in 1./2./3.; (1)/(2)/(3), or they were not. Thus, correction of the text often presupposed interpretation. Whenever a problem arose, we had to solve it consistently and familiarise our whole team with the solution so that they could all equally abide by it. We did so by using the browser OXYGEN 14 – human proofreaders would not have been able to reach consistency over 4,500 pages.

(13) Gie, (14) Goa, (15) Goe, (16) Goeth, (17) Goo, (18) Gooa, (19) Gowe, (20) Gu(e, (21) Guy, (22) Gwain(e, (23) Gwo(ə, (24) ?Yeand. [For further instances see II below.]
(1) Cum.¹, n.Yks.¹, w.Yks.⁴, Lan.¹, n.Lan.¹, ne.Lan.¹ (2) Nhb.¹ (s.v. Kaa). Wm. He gaas net to kirk, HUTTON *Bran New Wark* (1785) 454. w.Yks.¹, ne.Lan.¹ (3) N.Cy.¹ Nhb.¹ Gae doon the toon an' seek the milk. Dur.¹, n.Yks.¹² m.Yks.¹ Very well, mother; let him gae. w.Yks.¹ (4) Nhb.¹ (s.v. Kaa). s.Wm. Gah hēam (J.A.B.). ne.Yks.¹, m.Yks.¹ (5, 6) m.Yks.¹ (7) n.Cy. (HALL), Glo.¹ (8) m.Yks.¹, w.Yks.¹ (9) Sc. MURRAY *Dial.* (1873) 205. (10) w.Yks. WATSON *Hist.* *Hlfx.* (1775) 538; w.Yks.⁴ (11) N.Cy.¹ Cum.¹ He gez wid his feet breadd side furst. (12) e.Dev. Ai shall up an' geu voāth ta th' town, PULMAN *Sng. Sol.* (1860) iii. 2. (13) N.Cy.¹ (14) n.Yks. Don't goā oot te-day, LINSKILL *Betw. Heather and N. Sea* (1884) vi. m.Yks.¹ On I mud goa, CUDWORTH *Dial. Sketches* (1884) 16. (15, 16) Wxf.¹ (17) e.Lan.¹, Chs.¹ Stf.¹ I wunna goo. Der.² Wu't goo wi' mey. s.Not. (J.P.K.) Lin. But Parson a comes an' a goos, TENNYSON *N. Farmer, Old Style* (1864) st. 7. War.² *Introd.* 15. m.Wor. (J.C.), Suf. (F.A.A.) Sur.¹ I see him goo straight away across two fields. Sus. Well, gentlemen, I'll goo, I'll goo, EGERTON *Flk. and Ways* (1884) 55. I.W.¹ Wil. SLOW *Gl.* (1892). w.Som.¹ Dev. Zimon lad, thee mun goo to bed to onst, *Longman's Mag.* (Dec. 1896) 153. (18) w.Yks.²; w.Yks.⁴ Gooa abaht thee bisness. Der.¹ se.Wor. I have never heard any but old persons pronounce the word 'go' in this way. (19) Cum. Wull ta gowe wie me? (E.W.P.) (20) w.Yks. Guə, WRIGHT *Gram. Wndhll.* (1892) 143. Lan. Gut' Rachdaw weh a keaw, TIM BOBBIN *View Dial.* (1740) 11. Ken. No gu nigh de hosses, NAIRNE *Tales* (1790) 57, ed. 1824. (21) I.Ma. (S.M.) (22) Nhp.² Will you gwain wi' me? (23) Lan. Ut gwoes bith neame o' Kopper Nob, SCHOLES *Tim Gamwattle* (1857)

Figure 5.1 Extract from the entry of *GO*

5.2   The Task of Tagging

The vertical, rather than horizontal, text mode in XML was, in hindsight, an enormous advantage when our work focused on tagging. Here an important point was for us to keep all relevant units of text free from accidental disturbing factors. In a text sequence such as 'Yks., Lan. and e.Ang.', we had to make sure that *Yks.* and *Lan.* were tagged as counties, the comma as punctuation and *and* as 'surplus' (i.e. a superfluous unit) respectively, and *e.Ang.* as a region. When a compound was listed and its meaning was added, we had to use the comma between the two as a marker for the change of tags. In the case of phrases, it was sometimes difficult to know (except by philological *ad-hoc* interpretation) where a phrase, occasionally with punctuation marks in it, ended and where its definition, or eventually another phrase, started.

Like the orthographic correction work, the tagging would not have been possible manually, that is, word for word. Instead, we used one of the browsers available for XML-texts, OXYGEN 14. It allows the query routine XPATH, with which we worked initially, but it also provides various sophisticated find/ replace routines of its own, which we mainly used later. A precondition of our work with the OXYGEN browser was, however, that we had to split the

Figure 5.2 Find-replace command in Oxygen 14 (German version)

enormous amount of XML-text into smaller units to handle the huge numbers of its megabytes. Following our Trier partners in this point, we used the letters of the alphabet as a criterion of division, defining the *Dictionary* entries of A and the other 'smaller' letters as separate files and dividing the more substantial letters into four sections. The find/replace routine of OXYGEN allows the multiple truncation of data not only for individual files but also for the whole text, working off the given command for one letter-specific file after the other. In practice, we could also replace strings within multi-line data, defining the contextual variants of the strings as conditions. In the replacement box, the truncated parts of the 'find'-box can be reproduced by '$1/$2/$3' and so on, where the *numerus currens* reflects the order of the earlier asterisks or rather '(.*)' (in OXYGEN). Figure 5.2 shows an example of a moderately complex find-replace command, extending over three lines.

As mentioned in Chapter 4, many features of Wright's *EDD* had to be grasped by attributes rather than element tags due to the necessity of assimilating our initial tagging system to that of TEI. The attributes, for their part, also had to be adapted to the TEI system. There were moments when we regretted our readiness to follow TEI for various reasons. For example, TEI does not offer appropriate tags for compounds, derivations, phrases, and variants. Instead, these had to be defined as attributes. Moreover, many attributes had to be renamed. For example, the dates of year that could be found in entries marking the publication of sources were initially summarised by our two attributes *from* and *to*, marking the range from the earliest to the latest date. But it turned out that TEI does not 'know' the attributes *from* and *to* nor any other that would be suitable to express the notion of a time span. So we had to replace *from* and *to* with attribute names vaguely or hardly suggestive of their function: *prev*(ious) and *select*. There have been many such stopgap solutions so that the names of attributes, after the revision, became partly as intransparent as those of the element tags and equally difficult to work with and to remember.

When first confronted with this problem, I contacted one of the founder members of TEI, listing twelve main suggestions for improvement of the TEI element tags with reference to dictionaries. I abstained from adding proposals concerning attributes at this stage. The answer was formally polite but discouraging with regard to the time needed for taking notice of our suggestions. In order not to lose months, we continued our work with the TEI tags and attributes then available.

5.3   Survey of the Element Tags

The resulting extreme length and complexity of the element tags can be seen from the random selection of twenty-four tags in Table 5.1, which may stand for the tags' total of 1,265.

These tags and their frequency numbers[1] are based on our XML-versions of the texts **after** their adaptation to TEI. The first line of Table 5.1 illustrates this. TEI does not have a direct tag for citations, that is, Wright's passages of illustrative quotations. So we had to use a TEI-conforming cover-tag *dictScrap* (as it were, for some 'scrap' in the *Dictionary*), with the subordinate attribute CIT (for 'citation'). As was explained earlier, we capitalised this provisional tag to mark it as deviant in the TEI-system of element tags to be changed later into an attribute by the general and automatic transfer of the XML-text into a TEI-text. Likewise, *title_BIBLIO* consists of the makeshift TEI tag *title*, which stands for all kinds of source references, and the capitalised tag BIBLIO, which, while expressing the subtype of references to dialectological literature, does not exist as an element in TEI. Following Wright in this, we thought we should keep the references of the BIBLIO type separate from fictional and poetic texts. Again, capitalisation stands for the later transfer of the tag into an attribute.

To select the first four units of Table 5.1 for further demonstration concerning TEI: the XML-tag *dictScrap_CIT_title_BIBLIO*, with its immanent hierarchy expressed by the order of the tags, is changed by the automatic

---

[1] The given frequency figures may not all be up-to-date as we revised the tags in minor points until the very end of the project, i.e. October 2018.

Table 5.1 *Extract of the list of element tags needed for* EDD Online

dictScrap_CIT_title_BIBLIO_district_PREC_span_XNUM	3,381
dictScrap_CIT_title_BIBLIO_district_PREC_span_XNUM_ex	109
dictScrap_CIT_title_BIBLIO_district_PREC_surplus	1,574
dictScrap_CIT_title_BIBLIO_pc	8,827
dictScrap_CIT_title_BIBLIO_region_PREC	13,832
dictScrap_CIT_title_BIBLIO_region_PREC_pc	1,751
dictScrap_CIT_title_BIBLIO_region_PREC_span_NUM	502
dictScrap_CIT_title_BIBLIO_region_PREC_span_NUM_ex	48
dictScrap_CIT_title_BIBLIO_region_PREC_span_XNUM	93
dictScrap_CIT_title_BIBLIO_region_PREC_span_XNUM_ex	1
dictScrap_CIT_title_BIBLIO_region_PREC_surplus	9
dictScrap_CIT_title_BIBLIO_span_NUM	378
dictScrap_CIT_title_BIBLIO_span_NUM_ex	33
dictScrap_CIT_title_BIBLIO_span_XNUM	68
dictScrap_CIT_title_BIBLIO_surplus	13,607
dictScrap_CIT_title_CORRESP	49,994
dictScrap_CIT_title_CORRESP_pc	102,451
dictScrap_CIT_title_CORRESP_span_NUM	47
dictScrap_CIT_title_CORRESP_span_NUM_ex	2
dictScrap_CIT_title_CORRESP_span_XNUM	7
dictScrap_CIT_title_CORRESP_surplus	89
dictScrap_CIT_title_LIT	1,845
dictScrap_CIT_title_LIT_pc	205
dictScrap_CIT_title_LIT_surplus	149

transfer from XML to TEI into an expression using pointed brackets for the hierarchy:

```
<dictScrap type="CIT">
<title type="BIBLIO"/>
</dictScrap>
```

Even these three lines are sufficient to suggest that the hierarchical structures of TEI texts are practically unreadable, particularly because elements are nested within each other. The pointed brackets surround each element and its attribute(s). The slash (/) closes the element. The more further elements have to be opened (and closed) after the opening of a superior element, that is, the more embedded the given elements are, the less transparent the whole structure becomes for the human eye and brain. The computer, that is, TEI software, automatically provides the closure of opened elements and checks if and where any of the (limited) options of nesting are offended. We for our part initiated the automatism which changed provisionally capitalised tags into attributes, such as *type="CIT"*. The advantage of the attributes versus the element tags is that there is no prescriptive list of what they can contain – CIT is our own coinage. However, the names of attributes (*type* in the example just used) have to be selected from a fairly limited list of acceptable options, just as in the case of the element tags.

Our work with element tags and attributes demanded much patience on our part and was a repetitive process of creating new markers and of trying them out, with the aim of avoiding hapax tags. In the course of time, we have produced no less than 135 XML-versions of the *Dictionary* and 39 TEI versions. It was an enormous advantage for us to apply the permanent *post festum* corrections on the XML version and then to have this version transferred into TEI automatically. The query routines that had then to be implemented (with XQuery, JavaScript, CSS) could only function on the basis of TEI.

5.4   Survey of the Attributes

As mentioned, the pattern of attributes allows for a free choice of the abbreviation in quotation marks, that is of the 'value' of an attribute. Thus, instead of 'CIT' we could have used 'QUOTE'. But *type="xy"* is, though not the only one, still one of a very limited number of optional names/patterns for attributes prescribed by TEI. Moreover, the possible combinations of attribute names with elements are fairly limited, as is made clear on the 'googable' website of 'TEI coordinates'. As with the element tags, this prescriptive situation resulted in a number of somewhat intransparent attributes – for references to time ranges, for example, we had to use *prev* and *select*, rather than *from* and *to*, as mentioned earlier.

Notwithstanding this occasional lack of immediate transparency in the names of attributes, the selected list of them is somewhat revealing:

> ana="[for pages and years]" ('analysis')
> corresp='fauna'
> corresp='faunaD' [dialect]
> corresp='faunaE' [English]
> corresp='faunaT' [dialect term]
> corresp='flora'
> corresp='floraD'
> corresp='floraE'
> corresp='floraT'
> facs=[for coordinates] ('facsimile')
> n= [for the counting of the entries]
> next='true' [for page-breaking]
> prev=[for years (from)] ('previous')
> rend=[for periods of years]
> rend='bold'
> rend='capital'
> rend='italic'

rendition='endQuote'
rendition='endSource'
rendition='source'
rendition='startQuote'
rendition='startSource'
sameAs='[region]'
select='[for years (to)]'
select='ETYM'
sortKey='[for headword]'
style='abbr' ('abbreviation')
style='capital'
type='next'
value=[for whatever string][2]

This list, perhaps enigmatic at first sight, may demonstrate to the reader what attributes are good for. In a nutshell, they harbour collateral information, whereas the elements take care of mainstream information. We needed the attributes, with whatever name, for all those specific pieces of information that the *EDD* contains (beyond the information contained in the tags), from the different types of sources to the different types of dialectal reference (county/region/nation) and to different types of precision in this reference. A clear reference to, say, the county of Yorkshire (Yks.) was, accordingly, marked by *district_PREC*, or in TEI, *district type="PREC"*. Wright's less precise references, of the type 'in most parts of Yorkshire', were, as mentioned, not ignored but marked by the attribute *district type="FUZZY"*. By the same token, references to subdivisions of counties, in particular, cities, were marked by the attribute *type="PART"*, and those equipped with a direction, such as 'east'

---

[2] To quantify the names of attributes as of May 2017 (without their various values):

ana	2,255,798
corresp	30,596
facs	7,414,042
n	9,278,636
next	28,988
prev	25,145
rend	1,615,635
rendition	591,612
sameAs	152
select	34,180
sortKey	64,485
style	863,008
type	30,643 (in the letter A alone)
value	8,306,181

or 'nw.', were equally marked by the attribute *type="PART"*, to be kept apart on our interface as a separate group by their specific additional markers. On this basis, it will be possible for users to combine subsections of neighbouring counties, or for that matter, regions and nations.

A very special type of attribute was created by us to mark the beginning and end of quotations and of the given sources in the text. Quotations and sources are, in fact, often mixed in the citation blocks so that the software does not 'know' how to correlate data. Imagine a line-specific sequence such as the following:

Yks.1 / Quote / Wm.2 / Quote / Lan.1 / Nhb.2 / Lin.12

This schematic list (of a constructed case) implies that a source from Yorkshire and its quotation are followed by another source (Wm.2), again with a quotation taken from this source, and then followed by three sources without a quotation. The first two lines were marked by an initial attribute *startQuote="true"* and a final one *endQuote="true"*. The same applies to lines 3 and 4. The last three lines, however, are a block of mere sources, which we, therefore, marked by *startSource="true"* and *endSource="true"*. The point is that the sources do not all function on the same level, but have different 'referents' (to use today's text-linguistic terminology): Yks.1 and Wm.2 refer to their respective quotes only, but the subsequent three sources refer to the whole paragraphs preceding them. The antecedent could be a compound or a specific meaning of the entry concerned, or whatever. In any case, the immanent syntax of the units in the list had to be made clear for us to avoid misinterpreting Wright's data.

The necessity of clear referential attribution became obvious when we started writing our query commands. This was not a task that could simply be left to the programmer(s). On the contrary, the philologists in our team (Andrea Krapf and myself, but in the final phase mainly Andrea) had to do the greater part of this job. Of course, we had to decide what future users of *EDD Online* would wish to look for, and what criteria of combination would be desirable. Writing the query commands was a tough job, which deserves a subchapter of its own.

5.5   The Query Commands (in XPATH/XQUERY)

A fairly simple query command we worked out is presented in Figure 5.3.

XPath and XQuery are both languages that address special parts of an XML or TEI document – not primarily by referring to them as strings, but by focusing on their position in the hierarchy of the text or document. The hierarchy is mainly referred to in metaphorical terms of biological relationships: *child, parent, ancestor, descendant*, etc. For example, in the tag sequence used earlier *dictScrap_CIT_title_BIBLIO*, *dictScrap* and *title* have a parent-child relationship. The capitalised abbreviations CIT and BIBLIO are,

```
for $compTerm in
(//re[(@type="COMP")]/descendant::name/term[matches(text(),"^gan",'i')])
  let $comp:=$compTerm/ancestor::re[(@type="COMP")]
  let $entry:=$comp/ancestor::entry
  let $orth:=$entry/form/orth
  let $pos:=$entry/form/*/pos
  let $span:=$compTerm/preceding-sibling::span[1]
  let $spanValue:=replace($span,"[(]|[)]","")
  let $cit:=$comp/following-sibling::*[not(matches(name(),
'lb|gb|re'))][1][name()='dictScrap' and @change='CIT']
  let $spanCit:=$cit/descendant::span[@type="NUM"]
  let $spannext:=$spanCit[(replace(text(),"[(]|[)]","")= $spanValue][1]
  let $dialect:=$cit/(descendant::district | descendant::region | descendant::
country | descendant::title[(descendant::district|descendant::region|
descendant::country)])[matches(text(),".*",'i')][((preceding-sibling::span[@
type="NUM"][1]/preceding-sibling::*[1] [name()='span' and @type='NUM'])
 or (preceding-sibling::span[@type="NUM"][1])[text() = $spannext/text()]) ]
  let $dialect1:=$comp/district [preceding-sibling::name[1]/term[text() =
$compTerm][1]]
  let $dialect2:=$cit/(descendant::district | descendant::region | descendant::
country )[matches(text(),".*",'i')]
return
if ($spanValue="")
then
(if ($dialect2)
then
( $orth,
  $pos,
  $compTerm,
  $dialect1,
  $dialect2)
else())
else
(if ($dialect)
then
( $orth,
  $pos,
  $span,
  $compTerm,
$dialect1,
  $spannext,
  $dialect)
else())
```

Figure 5.3 XQuery command for finding compounds, their headwords and parts of speech, as well as the dialect areas they refer to

as attributes, likewise part of this relationship. Both elements and attributes are seen as 'nodes' of a 'tree', with the complete document as the highest node.

Figure 5.3 also contains some abbreviative signs of commands, such as // and @. The former means that all hierarchical levels are addressed, the latter is the 'at' sign well known from email addresses and, in fact, standing for 'attributes'. The dollar sign stands for variables. XQuery, building up on XPath and being the more complex language, also has operators, such as the equation mark (=) or its negation (!=). Moreover and above all, Figure 5.3 contains several functions of the type *if ... then ... else*.

As a philologist I would not think of trying here to explain these things to the full. As in natural languages, there are lexical and syntactic rules, to mention only these. As in natural language learning, we started with simple 'sentences', searches for headwords, and then built up on our newly acquired knowledge, with the query commands needed being longer and longer and increasing in complexity. The challenge was a permanent one because we could not simply hire XQUERY specialists.

One of the reasons for the complexity of such query formulas is that Wright's *EDD* is most ambitious in attributing linguistic features of headwords and other lexical items to dialectal areas, as in the case demonstrated in Figure 5.3. Another reason is the elaborate syntax and the diversity of rules available in XPATH and XQUERY. The challenge was, therefore, twofold and could only be met by our initial study of handbooks/internet help platforms, as well as constant teamwork, advice from our internal and occasionally external programmers and, finally, patience in a trial-and-error situation. Given these conditions, even 'monster formulas' longer than the one presented in Figure 5.3 were manageable.[3]

5.6   Data Management Plan

I abstain from trying to explain further technical aspects of our work in detail though they had a great share in our daily routine. Instead, the data management plan of Figure 5.4 (see colour version in the Appendix), in the form of a flow-diagram, may, by its mere complexity, testify to a large amount of tasks and software applications we were concerned with over the years. The flow chart was created by our web designer Martin Köll and myself (MM).

Some recursive loops are suggesting repetitive tasks in the chart. For example, the XML version of the *EDD* text had to be corrected and newly implemented again and again, as was mentioned earlier. Every time the computer/server had to work this off overnight. The chart of Figure 5.4 also vaguely reveals how our team members contributed to the work of our project, with the colours of the boxes standing for their individual achievements in terms of expertise, if not in terms of time invested. Notwithstanding this attribution to individuals, synergy was probably the most important factor in our work.

This chapter gives access to some of the main problems involved in our project work over the last ten years. Enough of this! As with theatrical or

---

[3] Two of the handbooks we used were: Harold and Means (2004) (*XML in a Nutshell*) (nearly 700 pages) and Walmsley (2007) (XQuery) (nearly 500 pages).

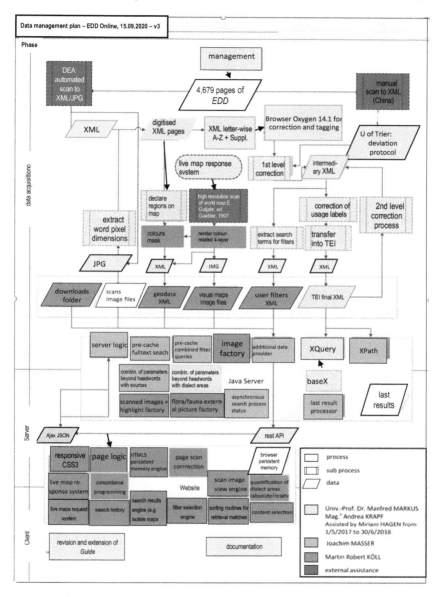

Figure 5.4 Data management plan of *EDD Online*

musical performances, spectators and audiences are generally less interested in rehearsals and the work behind the scenes (though some are), but in the 'show' itself. In our case, the 'show' is presented by the interface, that is, the screen with its icons, buttons and boxes by which users may communicate their wishes.

6 The Interface

Elementary Search Routines

6.1 Basic Search for Strings in Headwords

What can users search for on the interface?

Figure 6.1 shows us the basic version of the interface.

Clicking 'headword' (top left), or rather, leaving this default mode as it is, means working in the 'simple' mode, which allows the basic retrieval of a specific headword to be typed into the search box (top left). Moreover, if this box is left 'empty' (type in *), this mode allows for the retrieval of an alphabetical list of headwords in accordance with any of the filters, optionally activated on the right and documented by the search protocol (top right). For example, the string *humour* has been triggered by opting for one of the eight display filters (top right). These filters can be activated in isolation or combination, with the protocol always giving evidence of the possibly complex arrangement of filters. The user could, for example, search for humorous terms referring to women in England versus Scotland and/or Ireland. The default mode of presenting the results in the retrieval window is by headwords in their original sequential order of the *Dictionary*, with the keywords created by the activated filters subordinated by line insertion. As users may be interested in having either the headwords or the filter keywords in isolation and in alphabetical arrangement, different presentation modes (to be discussed in Section 6.2.8) are at their disposal. In any case, users can copy and paste the result lists of their queries.

Beyond this basic option of searching for headwords which fulfil certain filter conditions, the left half of the interface offers much more. In the following, we survey these additional options from top to bottom.

6.2 Retrieval Window (Simple Mode)

The options in the left half of the interface, including the 'retrieval window' and the headspace above it, are described in the following (Sections 6.2.1–6.2.8).

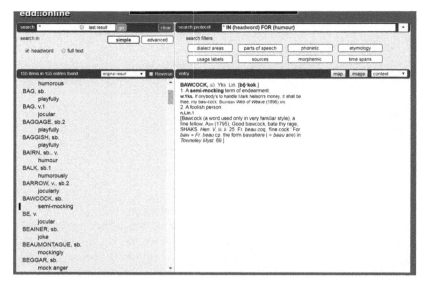

Figure 6.1 Headword query with activated filter 'humour' (selection from 140 headwords)

6.2.1   search

In the *search* box, users may put in strings, either as such (e.g. *house* means immanent truncation on either side) or explicitly truncated at the beginning or end of a string (**house* or *house**). If truncation is to be excluded, the search string has to be typed in double quotation marks (*"house"*). If users want to search for no particular string, but for all strings fulfilling the demands of any of the filters (to be discussed in detail in the following paragraphs), they just type in an asterisk (*), as mentioned earlier.

In quantitative terms, our search routine counts the items of retrieval in the dark green bar above the retrieval list (in Figure 6.1: 155 items). If something else than headwords is the object of a query, then the number of the headwords involved is added, in addition to the number of items found. The retrieval list is stopped if the number of items surpasses 5,000. However, all items beyond that limit, up to 100,000, are counted. Quantitatively challenging queries may end up in your computer's breakdown due to the limits of our server or of the user's browser. If the *clear* button does not react any more, close *EDD Online* and re-start it after a short while. However, before the breakdown, quantitatively demanding queries may also trigger the pop-up question whether the user wants to stop or continue the started query, with either option viable. The continuation is worth trying out for up to three times.

6.2.2   last result *(within Search Box)*

This button allows piggy-back queries, i.e. searches within the sub-set of the results of a previous search, thus encouraging searches of greater complexity or 'second-thought' searches. For example, a search for compounds plus filter 'all counties in England' produces too many hits to be manageable so that the user may wish to impose more restrictive filters, such as 'Yorkshire' alone plus the label/frequency filter 'common'. Note that the 'last result' button only allows second-thought queries within the set of headwords (or rather: their entries) previously found so that a posterior change of the parameter (in this case: of *compound*) and a change or addition of filters are only possible within these limits. In other words, if the first search has referred to a special string, say $a*$, the follow-up query can only be triggered by cancelling this specificity. So instead of again searching for $a*$, the user should be searching for $*$, that is, anything fulfilling the previously defined conditions plus the conditions then added. Another example would be the *last-result* combination of a primary search for word-initial *ha-* (i.e. *ha**) in the headwords with a secondary search for $a*$ in the parameter of *variants*. This would be the way to trace *h*-dropping (to be discussed in Section 7.6).

The *last-result* option can also be applied repeatedly, which allows for an enormous increase in the number of possibilities when shaping one's queries. This useful tool will further be demonstrated in selected applications in Chapter 8.

6.2.3   *go*

The orange button *go* starts the query. Note that the computer needs some seconds for 'grasping' query compositions before the *go* button reacts. It stands to reason that *go* presupposes some string or the asterisk to be searched for. If the search box is empty, the *go* button responds with the answer 'Please enter search term'.

6.2.4   *clear*

The *clear* button deletes whatever has been searched for and retrieved previously. This removal includes maps, entry images and whatever else has been activated in a previous query.

6.2.5   *simple/advanced*

The activated button of the optional two modes appears in bold. As an alternative to *simple*, *advanced* opens a new window with possible queries

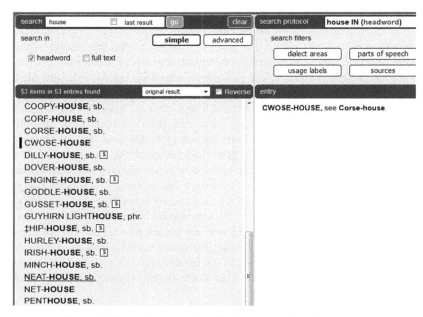

Figure 6.2 Search for *house* (implicitly truncated), with opening of the cross-referential entry CWOSE-HOUSE

that are more specific than those for headwords or within the full text. We may, for example, wish to search within *definitions* for semantically interesting strings or for phrases (idioms). These 'advanced' options will be discussed in detail in Section 6.2.8. As they are not visible to users right after starting *EDD Online*, they may appear to be less important. Far from it. They are an essential asset of *EDD Online*.

6.2.6   headword

This button opens the basic mode of searching for headwords (or 'lemmas'). Note that some of Wright's headwords are not lexemes in the modern linguistic sense, but phonemes (very rarely, particularly at the beginning of the letter *A*), bound morphemes, derivations, compounds, combinations, and phrases. Almost all headwords are accompanied by their part or parts of speech, for example, *GO, v.* The headwords with no such part-of-speech marker are variants accompanied by cross references, as illustrated in Figure 6.2.

Figure 6.2 also demonstrates two more points: the now integrated lemmas of the *Supplement*, marked by S-boxes, and entries of the *Supplement* classified by Wright as unsatisfactorily authorised, identified in the *Supplement* by a double dagger (as in the case of HIP-HOUSE).

6.2.7   *full text*

This is a mode to be recommended only for tentative queries. For example, if users are undecided about the location of their query word in an entry or if they wish to know if a string or letter exists at all within the *Dictionary*. This mode only reproduces the search strings without the entries they belong to and irrespective of context. However, a click on one of the strings shown in the retrieval list produces the entry window with that string in the context of its entry.

Full text does not allow any combination with any other parameter or with a filter. But as with the headwords, this mode allows truncation.

6.2.8   Original result *Box and* Reverse *Button*

The white box in Figure 6.2 saying 'original result' by default presents the matches of a search in the original order of the *Dictionary*. With headwords this, by and large, alphabetical order seems the most natural mode. But other sorting modes are also available in this box. For example, in searches for compounds the 'original' mode is that of the alphabetised headwords concerned, whereas the user will probably prefer an A–Z order of the compounds themselves, taken out of their headword context. In addition, the *Reverse* button next to the *original result* box permits a reverse sorting order, with findings arranged alphabetically as seen from their ends (which may be of interest for suffix or rhyme-word studies).

There are also various other sorting modes that isolate the retrieved columns and quantify both types and tokens provided by a query. This additional quantification of retrievals is, of course, of no interest in the case of mere headword searches because with these the number of retrieved headwords and the sometimes slightly deviant number of the entries involved are always provided after queries anyway – see the detailed discussion of this information box below (in Section 6.2, following Figure 6.8). The quantifications are always defined column specifically. If there is only one column, that of the headwords, without dialects or any of the other filters involved, there is no need of re-sorting.

Things are different when the query result implies two or more columns, that is, when the advanced query modes and the results of filters are involved. For

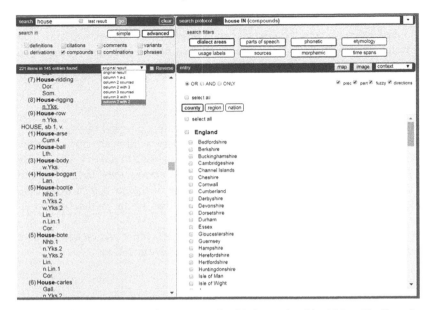

Figure 6.3 Search for *compounds* with *house* (world-wide), with all sorting options opened and the *column 3 with 2* mode highlighted (though not activated)

these cases, we have implemented sophisticated combinations, for example, *column 2 with 3* and *column 3 with 2*, where 'column' refers to the hierarchy level of the parameters and filters involved in a query. The number and types of the sorting options depend on the complexity of a combined query. In Figures 6.3–6.8, the main sorting modes are illustrated by the (implicitly truncated) string *house* in compounds, with all counties worldwide activated. Users are, however, requested to try out these sorting options for themselves to appreciate their enormous potential.

It is, therefore, clear that users of *EDD Online* in their searches can focus on many different items of dialectal language according to their interests. Before we leave the left (retrieval) half of the interface, mention should finally be made of the counting mechanism in the dark bar above the retrieval window. In Figures 6.3–6.6, 221 compounds with *house* are listed, attributed to 145 entries. While the dialectal areas concerned are automatically added here, they are not used as a restrictive filter. This is only the case in Figures 6.7 and 6.8 where the dialect filter was limited to (all) counties, with regions and nations excluded, so that the numbers of the items and entries found are lower than before (202 items in 131 entries).

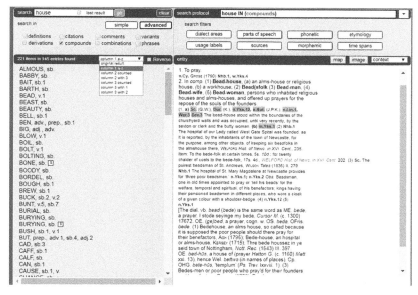

Figure 6.4 Identical with search in Figure 6.3, but with headwords sorted A–Z

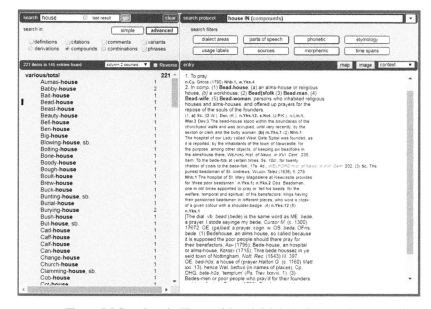

Figure 6.5 Search as in Figures 6.3 and 6.4, but with sorted compounds
(*column 2 counted*)

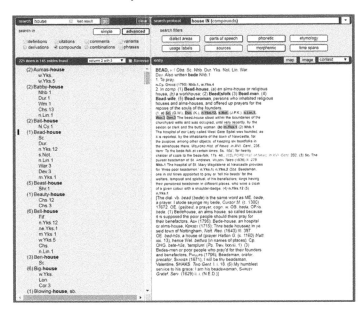

Figure 6.6 Search as in Figures 6.3–6.5, but with sorted compounds plus their dialects/counties (*column 2 with 3*)

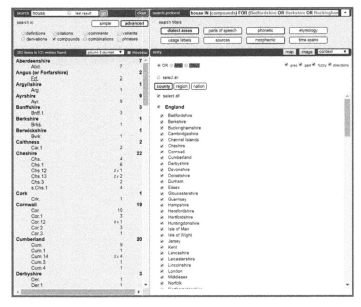

Figure 6.7 Search as in Figures 6.3–6.6, but with the filter of dialects/counties added and the dialects sorted and counted as tokens and types (*column 3 counted*)

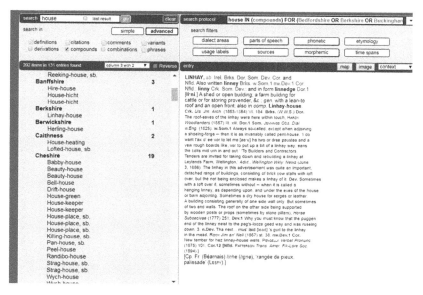

Figure 6.8 Repetition of previous search 6.7, but with sorted dialects/counties plus compounds attributed to them (*column 3 with 2*)

6.3 Entry Window and the Role of Filters

6.3.1 Survey

As can be seen from the screenshots of Figures 6.3–6.8, the options on top of the right half of the interface (above the entry window) are as follows.

search protocol: This box automatically displays all major steps of queries, including the *advanced* query routines and the filters (excluding sub-filters, however). This tool is particularly useful in the case of complex queries with different filters (Figure 6.9).

As one can see, the box of the protocol/memo at the top is too small to grasp all the counties, but when the user moves the mouse into the protocol box, the complete list of the counties pops up (Figure 6.10).

At the right end of the protocol box, there is a memory function – an arrow for recalling previous search protocols.

The big group of the search filters allows for activating (in the order listed on the interface from left to right): (1) *dialect areas*, (2) *usage labels*, (3) *parts of speech*, (4) *sources*, (5) *phonetic*, (6) *morphemic*, (7) *etymology* and (8) *time spans*. As shown in Figure 6.3, some of the filters have a small red frame –

Figure 6.9 Search for *house* combined with filter 'all counties of England', with the beginning of the list of counties opened

these are the filters thus marked to be unacceptable in the case of a given parameter (e.g. *compounds*). All the other filters are compatible with each other and with the given parameter.

The following sections of this chapter discuss all the filters, irrespective of their (non-)acceptability in special cases, in turn and in detail.

6.3.2   Dialect Areas

'Area' is the cover term for 'county', 'region' and 'nation'. The counties, like Yorkshire (Yks.), are arranged nation-wise, with England followed by (the whole of) Ireland, Scotland, Wales, Australia, Canada and the USA. This order was favoured, notwithstanding the criterion of the alphabet, in line with the assumed frequency. Note that some historically extant counties (and 'states' respectively) have not been mentioned in our interface lists, particularly in the case of Ireland, Wales and the USA, for the simple reason that these counties and states have no matches in the entire *EDD*. However, the lists of counties also include individually named sub-sections, in particular, cities and, occasionally, rivers, to be activated by *part*, and also *fuzzy* references, such as 'some parts of x' or 'west of x in y'. Moreover, some of the precise references to counties are specified by directions of the compass: north, southeast and so on. In a headline of the dialect filter, we have, therefore, provided four sub-filters: *prec(ise)*, *part*, *fuzzy* and *directions* (to be seen in Figure 6.10).

The four sub-filters are valid for all those counties that have been selected by users. The default mode for the use of the four sub-filters, however, is to have them all included. If users want to limit their query to the precise data of dialect attribution, they have to keep *prec* marked and annul the other three options.

The list of counties in our interface follows Wright's terminology and generally represents the political situation of the late nineteenth century. The important county reform of 1974 is, of course, irrelevant. The Isle of Man, though never a 'county' in the strict sense of the word (but a self-governing British Crown dependency), has, however, to simplify matters, been listed with the English counties.

The relationship between the three types of area (*county*, *region* and *nation*) and the four modes of precision/sub-filters (*prec*, *fuzzy*, *part*, and *directions*) is such that queries for all areas allow for a combination with all four precision

Figure 6.10 Pop-up window of the search protocol, with all English counties selected

modes. However, *region* and *nation* mainly produce *precise* or *fuzzy* results, but no output for both *part* and *directions*.[1]

The second area-group, *regions*, such as *w.Cy.* (for 'West Country'), is generally structured in the interface in the same way as that of the counties, with England, Ireland and so on at the top. However, the third area group, *nations* (such as the USA), is much shorter than the county lists and, therefore, simply alphabetically arranged, without any sub-classification. Note that after the eleven nations, from Australia to Wales, another group, COLONIAL, had to be added for occasional references in the *EDD* to the West Indies and other nineteenth-century colonies of the UK.[2] The West Indies are also listed under *regions* as the only sub-division of COLONIAL.

All three types of areas, *counties*, *regions* and *nations*, can be combined with each other, by either 'OR' or 'AND' in the Boolean sense. The operator ONLY is also technically possible, though not always advisable (to be discussed in the following paragraphs). The three options are provided in the respective headline of the entry window (see the protocol in Figure 6.11), which shows the result of a query for headwords in both Ireland and the USA (i.e. logical AND).

As the retrieval window on the left in Figure 6.11 and also the protocol on top of the interface show, the logic of this query in the Boolean sense of AND is that the strings searched for have to be testified to in both the USA and Ireland. We can see from the selected example BEAL that the references to the two nations at issue may be anywhere in the entries. Note that the OR- versus AND-option equally applies to the two different levels of dialect attribution: (1) the sub-filters (nation/region/county) in relation to each other; (2) the keywords within these sub-filters, no matter which sub-section of the sub-filters they belong to so that Yorkshire can be combined with Edinburgh, but also with any region or non-UK nation. The only limitation is that OR or AND are always valid for all activated features alike. A combination of the type *(Ireland)* **AND** *(USA* **OR** *Amer.)* is not possible in this mode, but can be achieved using the *last-result*-button (mentioned in Section 6.2.2). *Qua* filter, however, *dialect area*s can be combined with any other filter, such as *parts of speech* or *usage labels*, where the implicit logic for the filters is always

---

[1] The reason simply is that *part* and *direction* are by definition sub-divisions: within the three-level system of the areas, it only makes sense to subdivide the smallest type of areas, the *counties* (e.g. by referring to cities within them), but a sub-division of *regions* would simply equal a reference to the *counties*, and a sub-division of the *nations* (e.g. of the UK) would take us back to the *regions*.

[2] In the fifty-six references to 'colonial English', there is only one further specification (to the West Indies).

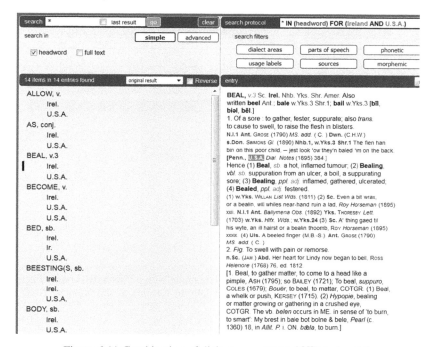

Figure 6.11 Combination of dialect areas (*USA* **AND** *Ireland*) for any headword

Boolean AND and where the sub-filters and keywords can be related by either OR or by AND. This possible combination of OR and AND is illustrated in Figure 6.12.

As mentioned, the filter *dialect areas*, unlike the other filters, provides a third option: ONLY. When this is activated, users retrieve search items that are dialectally restricted to one nation, region, or county, respectively. This ONLY function is a helpful tool for creating glossaries of area-specific dialect words that were, according to Wright, not traced anywhere else. The normal way to use this option is, of course, by searching in one particular area of interest. Our interface, however, allows for simultaneous ONLY searches in two or more areas, for example, counties, as well. The interface then nicely lists in a row the unique words or strings for the counties involved.

Users are, however, advised not to trust the results of ONLY searches blindly. There may be counter-productive additions in the text that have not been recognised as such. For example, the entry A-DAYS is attributed to 'e. An. and var. dial'. Our software has only grasped 'e.An.', but ignored the

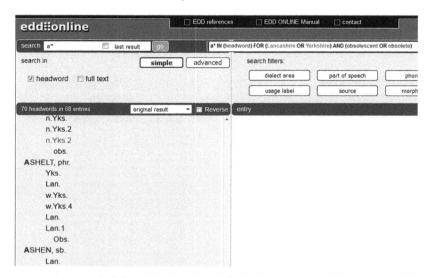

Figure 6.12 Search for headwords beginning with *a**, with two county filters and two label filters combined internally by OR, but as sub-filters by AND (see protocol box)

fuzzy rest. While the match lists of ONLY queries, then, have to be seen with a grain of salt, 'fuzzy rests' of the kind just mentioned are extremely rare.

The (lack of) compatibility of the different filter levels (i.e. filters, sub-filters and keywords in them) and their complex relation to the three Boolean operators invites a short summary. Users are generally advised to remember the following rules:

The eight **main filters** can be combined with each other by AND only (OR would not make sense). Accordingly, a search for interjections (*parts of speech*) in, say, Yorkshire would only provide entries with markers of both criteria in them (i.e. combined by Boolean AND).

The **sub-filters** of *dialect areas*, such as *county,* can be combined with the other sub-filters (in *region/nation*) by both OR and AND, but once the user has decided for one of these options, the same logic prevails for eventual multiple keywords (*Yorkshire* plus *Lancashire*).

It may be said in advance here that within the main filters, things had to be settled differently from case to case. While the filter *dialect areas* has the two Boolean options as explained (OR and AND), as well as the option ONLY, *usage labels*, with its eight sub-filters, has only AND. P*arts of speech* has no Boolean option at all – there are no sub-filters, but only, on a lower level, the keywords for the word classes.[3] Likewise, all the other filters lack Boolean sub-options, except for *etymology*, which again has the three options of the dialect distribution at its disposal: OR, AND and ONLY.

By contrast, the sub-filters of the *usage labels* all have keywords (as sub-sub filters, so to speak), which, for their part, in searches can be combined by either OR or AND. Thus, in the usage label *frequency*, one could search in one go for *obsolescent* and (i.e. Boolean OR) *obsolete* items. The combination of such a search with any keywords of another sub-filter (within *usage labels*), for example, of *semantics* follows the same logic: sub-filters, here *frequency* and *semantics*, and single keywords within them, automatically combine by AND; the keywords within these sub-filters, if there is more than one, combine by OR or AND, as marked by the user. We could, thus, ask for *obsolescent* OR *obsolete* items which (AND!) refer to children OR women.

By and large, AND-combinations below the level of the filters should be used sparingly and with a special focus in mind.

Users not at all interested in **specific** dialect areas, but, for example, in surveys concerning certain topical domains, such as figurative language or flora, may wish to cover **all** dialects at a time. For such users, the headline button *select all* can be activated, both on the general level and on the specific levels of either *nations* or *regions* or *counties*. If there are, however, more than 5,000 matches, our software stops providing further entries. Instead, the occurrences are simply counted up to 100,000. To avoid a breakdown of the server, users are advised not to challenge the server unduly by raising too general questions. The *clear*-button will, however, usually allow a query to be started from scratch. If the server reacts 'stubbornly' or as if it is having a 'nervous breakdown', close and re-start the whole program.

Dialect areas concerned by a particular query can be visualised by the *map*-button (on the right of the entry window). This button prompts either a map of the UK or of the world, depending on which areas have been found in the retrieval window. When users click on the headword, all the areas concerned by that headword are highlighted on the map. Note that these areas are, in principle, not identical with the ones listed under that headword in the retrieval window because these areas of the retrieval list are often a mere subset, depending on your more or less restrictive filtering.

In addition to the illustration of occurrence by maps, there is another device of assistance. Given that the abbreviations of dialect areas will not be familiar to many users and that exact geographical knowledge cannot generally be taken for granted, a click on a particular area triggers a separate window that zooms this area of the map. If, however, users have searched for, say, *compounds* and have

---

[3] The AND on top refers to the filter *parts of speech* as a whole in relation to the other main filters, e.g. *dialect areas*.

also selected *dialect areas,* the entry window will show three columns, the headwords in the left column, the compounds in the middle and the dialect areas in the right column. In this case, the map will selectively show all the dialect areas attributed to the compound of interest. By contrast, a click on the headword highlights all areas of distribution of the headword as a whole, as mentioned earlier. We can, thus, compare the distribution of a headword as such versus that of a particular type of word formation based on that headword.

Since dialect distribution is generally conditioned by geography, we have, in addition to the normal outline maps of the counties and of the other regional subdivisions, also implemented a physical and a hybrid map. We have, moreover, equipped our map of the UK with the blue lines showing the rivers. It is, therefore, easy for users to correlate dialect distribution with rivers and mountain ranges. For example, the Pennines are likely to be the main historical motivation for the distinction of the Yorkshire versus Lancashire dialect (as perhaps also for the famous War of the Roses).

Alternative physical maps would not have made much sense for the English-speaking countries overseas: North America, the West Indies, South Africa, Australia and New Zealand. The reason is that local geography hardly played a role when most of the federal states of North America, Australia and the other countries mentioned fell under colonial administration. Furthermore, Wright refers to the USA, Canada and also Australia mostly as a whole, except some of the New England states, Nova Scotia and Newfoundland, on the one hand, and New South Wales and Victoria, on the other hand. For the remainder, Wright's information on the West Indies, South Africa and New Zealand is patchy.

Our zoom gadget, just mentioned, also works for the world map, but we have installed it mainly for users to better visualise the outline map of the UK, with its often small areas and with the traditional three-letter abbreviations filled in. They will not all be readily available to present-day users.[4] The zoom-box, therefore, also provides both a county's abbreviation and its full name. Figure 6.13 demonstrates this gadget, together with the outline map. The zoom-box is a smart-tag device, popping up according to the cursor's position on the map.

In addition to the three types of maps mentioned earlier, there is a fourth option, for mapping quantities of dialectal occurrence. The maps of this type do not illustrate the existence or non-existence of one particular item in terms of geographical distribution, but rather the frequencies of dialectal references, for example, to counties on the basis of retrieval lists. This quantifying search

---

[4] Since the later twentieth century there have been reforms in the British county structure in favour of smaller units and a larger role of the big cities. Leeds, for example, was part of Yorkshire's West Riding, but is now an autonomous authority.

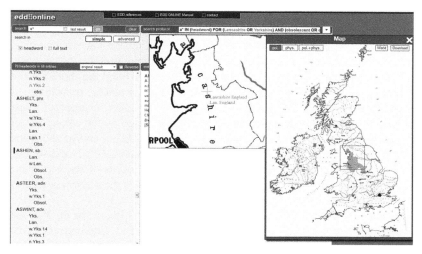

Figure 6.13 Highlighting Lancashire with pop-up zoom

routine will certainly be needed for many research issues, for example, in *phonetics*, where areal overlaps of usage are to be expected.

While quantification of dialectal features is generally difficult (see the complex suggestions made by dialectometry, e.g. Göbl (1982), and the detailed discussion in Chapter 9), a county-specific measuring of features, with counties contrasted with each other, also seems to make sense based on the numbers of references related to the given county. The simple formula used here is that the more areal evidence there is in the *EDD* for a particular feature, the more it is established in the areas concerned.

We have implemented several modes of quantity measuring: the first mode shows the geographical distribution of an item irrespective of the sum total of references to the areas concerned, but simply in relation to the other areas addressed in a query. This 'absolute' mode will certainly demonstrate that Wright did not have the intention of balancing out his references to areas: Yorkshire and its Ridings are his favourites, whereas the Welsh counties, except for Pembrokeshire, have been greatly neglected. However, given this obvious lack of balance, we have built in a few options of a second type which calculate retrieved frequencies in relation to the total numbers of area references concerned. This is the normalisation running in the background. Accordingly, when the high-frequency figure of a search item in Yorkshire is related to the high number of all references to that county in the *EDD*, its overwhelming dominance on the map is substituted by its adjusted (i.e. normalised) share. The first sub-mode of this normalised measuring is in percentages (%), the second in per thousand (‰), and a third in relation to 10,000 (‰0). It depends on the question which of these three sub-options is best suited to illustrate the occurrence of features across counties. Users have to find out for themselves which option they prefer.

The ratios worked out by our software in the background are, both for the 'absolute' and 'relative' or normalised figures of occurrences, transferred to our quantitative maps. The maps are designed as so-called cheropleth maps with ten colours. The meaning of the colours is explained by the colour bar on the accompanying legend. In general, each colour on the bar and on the maps stands for a tenth of the difference between the quantities of occurrence. Figure 6.14 illustrates the number of *sc*-initial dialect words of English counties in absolute terms, whereas Figure 6.16 demonstrates the important role of the normalisation of these figures.

As mentioned, 'absolute' here means that the figures given for the various counties are only related to the sum total listed at the end. In the case of *sc**, this sum total amounts to 7,275 areal references. The exact figure of occurrence for each county pops up if the user moves the cursor to a particular county. This tool is shown in Figure 6.15.

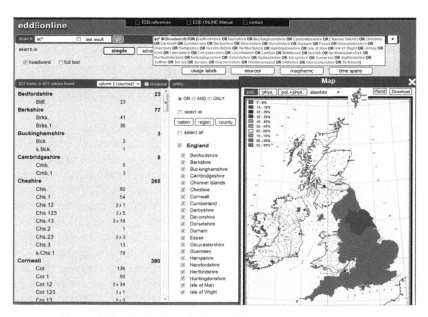

Figure 6.14 Distribution of *sc**-words in England (absolute figures)

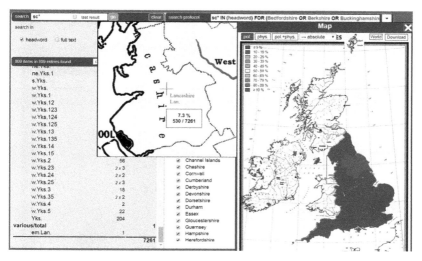

Figure 6.15 Share of Lancashire shown in pop-up window (in percentage of the number of all English counties)

The (rounded-up) percentage figure (7.3 per cent) is, of course, only of interest when compared to the figures for other counties. Cambridgeshire, for example, has 0.1 per cent, Leicestershire 1.4 per cent and so on. The problem of this mode of quantifying, however, is twofold: the percentage figures depend on how many counties and which ones are included in a query.[5] Above all, this mode has the disadvantage that, due to the extreme predominance of Yorkshire in the *EDD*, all the other counties are equally ranked as lowest-level cases (i.e. under 10 per cent). In principle, there are two ways of avoiding this. (1) The user excludes Yorkshire from the query so that the sum total of occurrences is drastically reduced. But this is a rather *ad-hoc* solution. Moreover, Yorkshire is not the only favourite county in the *EDD*. (2) A better way of getting evidential results in the case of survey queries (as with 'all English counties' as a search criterion) is the mode mentioned earlier, that is, the numbers of occurrence are related to the overall figures stored in the background for each individual county so that Yorkshire loses its predominance. This second search mode, with figures calculated in per thousand (*per mille*), is generally recommended. Figure 6.16 illustrates its effects.

---

[5] Trivial to say, this is like the percentage figures for political parties. If these fail to reach the minimum percentage of voters in elections, the share of the others in the distribution of parliamentary seats may substantially change.

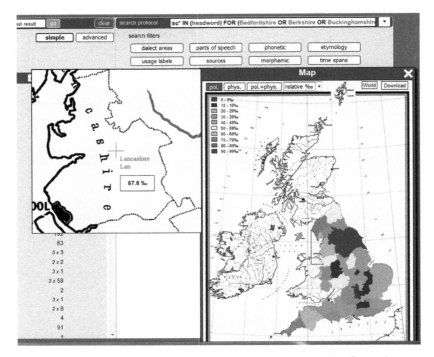

Figure 6.16 Distribution of *sc**-words in England (relative figures in per thousand), with a zoom on Lancashire

Figure 6.16 attests to an optimal mean variation between 1 and 100 per thousand, using all the colours in the legend bar of the map. As the pop-up window shows, Lancashire now has 67.6 ‰. The formula for this type of 'normalised' quantification is

$n_1 \times 1{,}000/n_t$,

where n_1 is the quantity of occurrences of a given county and n_t the sum total of references to this county (stored by our software). The number 1,000 is the multiplicator for acquiring per-thousand figures.

Other queries are certainly imaginable, demanding a calculation on the 10,000, rather than on the percent or per-thousand, scale. Which of the three sub-modes is most suitable depends on the type of query. Generally, frequent items, such as cases of *h*-dropping (see the analysis below), will go for a percentage quantification. Rare features, by contrast, are probably best mapped if related to 10,000 as a *quorum*. The researcher's aim should always be to get good dispersal.

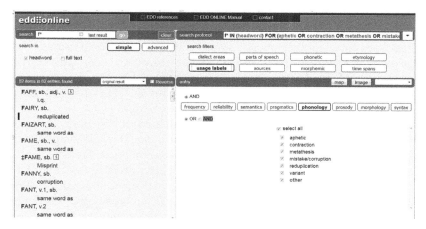

Figure 6.17 The subdivision of the filter *usage labels,* with *phonology* (all keywords) opened

The many ways of dialectal areas functioning as search filters will be further illustrated by examples of study issues in Section 8.3.

6.3.3   Usage Labels

The search filter **usage labels** reflects the *EDD*'s abundant application of usage information. Usage labels are numerous not only as tokens, but also as types, with the information ranging from frequency to pragmatics. Wright did not, of course, know terms such as *pragmatics* in the modern linguistic sense, but his reference to special user groups, for example, women, children, and members of various crafts, has caused us to include pragmatics in addition to other linguistic categories. Here is the complete list of the types of labels: *frequency, reliability, semantics, pragmatics, phonology* (including phonetics), *prosody, morphology* and *syntax.* Figure 6.17 illustrates these sub-filters, as they appear on the *EDD* interface.

It was not easy for us to trace concrete cases of labels in the *EDD* text, particularly in view of the fuzzy edges between language and habits of behaviour (for example, concerning children in playgrounds). We have done our best to keep linguistically relevant pieces of information completely and correctly apart from cultural ones, but then the two often go hand in hand, and I am not convinced that we have reached absolute perfection in the task of separating them. Whenever we have found Wright to be too verbose in his labelling style (e.g. when a word is 'used as a quasi-archaic word by the poets of the 19th century') to allow for easy extraction of a keyword without

over-generalisation, we have identified the labels by marking a typical introductory formula that generally precedes them. In the example just given, the
phrase 'used as' could function as a syntactic marker for users to interpret the
subsequent text for themselves. In the interface list of keywords, passages of
this unpredictable kind were subsumed under the last item of the keyword list,
called *other*. This 'leftover' subtype encourages browsing, not only in the label
type of *pragmatics*, but also in *semantics* and *phonology*.

There was, of course, much overlapping, as in modern linguistics, between
different linguistic disciplines/categories. The label *dim.* (for 'diminutive'), for
example, has morphological, semantic and pragmatic implications (cf. Markus
2010b). While we have generally tried to take a clear decision in our attribution, some multi-filter keywords have remained ambiguous, *diminutive* being
one of them in that it is listed in both pragmatics and morphology.[6] We have,
however, always tagged individual passages of the *Dictionary* one way or
another. As users can easily combine categories and thus still find those that
have several usage 'habitats', it is up to them to critically review our classification and to draw their own conclusions.

To keep the lists of keywords, for example, in the sub-menu of pragmatics,
in moderate length, we have normalised the relevant terms of the *Dictionary* so
that sometimes half a dozen or more strings (such as *emphasis, emph.,
emphatic, emphatically, emphasise, stressed, stress, highly stressed,* etc.) were
reduced to just one (*emphatic*). This principle was generally applied whenever
necessary. For example, the list of semantic features presented to the users of
our interface is also a normalised one. While Wright was in many ways ahead
of his time, his scholarly terminology was, from a modern point of view,
sometimes rudimentary and often tentative, and, in his use of abbreviations and
grammatical forms, inconsistent.

The complexity of Wright's labelling has resulted in our eight types of
labels and the more than a hundred tokens behind them (as with the variants of
emphatic listed above). Moreover, there is an unpredictable syntax. To illustrate this, it is not reliably predictable what exact position a marker such as *obs.*
(for 'obsolete') has in the text in relation to the unit(s) in its surroundings, be it
a headword of an entry as a whole or a specific compound, phrase, variant,
citation, comment or whatever else within an entry. Sometimes the label
precedes its referent, sometimes it follows it, sometimes contiguously and
sometimes at a distance. We persistently tried to grasp the variable relationships between the usage labels and their referents, but these pairings also

---

[6] In the earlier versions of *EDD Online*, it was partly attributed to semantics, but given the paucity
of the examples concerned, we later omitted this type.

turned out to depend on the individual labels. So we cannot guarantee but only hope that each label found in a query has correctly been referred to the string type it belongs to. For individual cases, however, users can always easily find out about this specific relationship between units of an entry by checking contexts in the entry window in the right half of the interface, starting from the highlighted label.

Figure 6.17 includes the sub-filter *reliability*, the second from the left. This needs some explanation. It was only recently (in 2018) added to the other seven label filters, the main reason being the addition of the *Supplement* to the *EDD*. The three keywords in *reliability* are: *Suppl.: uncertain; Suppl.: certain;* and *questionable*. The former two are due to Wright having marked some of the entries in the *Supplement* with a double dagger, namely those which he felt did not have 'sufficient authority' from his sources. These double-daggered cases are those that we have marked as 'uncertain'. To turn the argument on its head, this means that the remaining entries in the *Supplement* are the 'certain' ones (by far the majority). *Questionable* is the keyword applied to all entries or strings within entries, both in the *Supplement* and the *Dictionary* proper, that are marked by a question mark, to indicate that Wright was not completely sure of the information given.

These three keyword options allow users to easily retrieve (a) all *Supplement* entries, (b) the sub-set of all uncertain or certain entries in the *Supplement* and (c) all questionable cases in the whole *EDD* (based on Wright's own judgement). There is plenty of 'food' here for thought and further research. Thus, one could select all 'uncertain' and/or 'questionable' cases and nurture the ambition to complement Wright's knowledge.

Nowhere in the *EDD* does Wright give a satisfactory explanation for his criteria of brandmarking some of the entries as dubious cases. In a detailed analysis (Markus 2019b), which needs not be repeated here, I have come to the conclusion that, rather than one particular motive, a whole set of criteria played a role for Wright's decisions.

6.3.4   Parts of Speech

In this filter, a list of twenty-one word classes, from noun to interjection, is available. 'Hybrids' of word classes, however, have been split: in 'verbal noun' and 'adverbial adjective', for example, *noun* and *adjective* have been classified as word classes, but the specifying adjectival attributes *verbal* and *adverbial* have been marked by the tag *grammar* and can be traced via the label *LABELSYN*, that is, in one of the labels offered as options (mainly in *syntax*).

The keywords used in the *parts-of-speech* filter generally follow Wright's traditional terminology, with *phrase* disputably included in the canon of *parts*

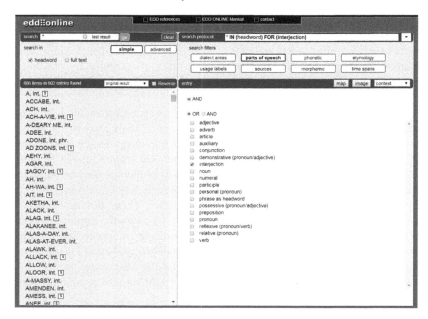

Figure 6.18 Search for all headwords that are interjections

of speech. We have opted against hierarchising the keywords so that *pronoun* is linearly listed with *reflexive, relative* and other types of pronouns. This seemed advisable because Wright, instead of using the technical terms 'relative/personal pronoun', sometimes refers to 'relative/personal adjectives' or uses 'relative', 'personal' etc. as grammatical terms in some other way (e.g. 'relative sense', 'the relative').

To select interjections as a part of speech which I understand to be particularly typical of the spoken language of dialect (cf. Markus 2015), Figure 6.18 shows part of the surprisingly long list of them (806 matches) after a search for this word class without any further specification.

6.3.5   Sources

Generally, we have had problems of identifying authors and texts within three categories of sources. The initials of correspondents were often either ambiguous or hard or impossible to identify. For the two types of *dialectal* and *literary sources*, it was sometimes difficult to impossible to decide which of the two groups a work or author belonged to.

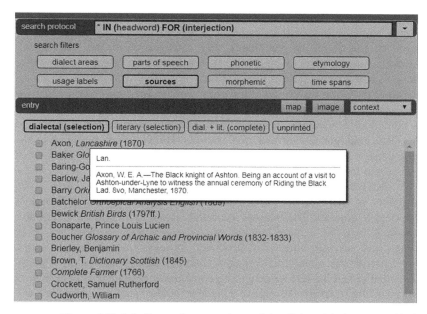

Figure 6.19 Sub-filters of *sources*, here of the *dialectal (selection)*, with the
full title of a specific source reference opened and highlighted by a smart tag[7]

Three types of sources have been kept apart, generally in line with Wright's
own practice. Dialectologically informative sources have been tagged as
title_BIBLIO, unprinted works and information provided by individual helpers
have been marked by the usually three initials of their names and have been
tagged as *title_CORRESP*. Finally, literary works have been referred to by
author and/or abbreviated title and are marked in the XML text of *EDD Online*
by the tag *title_LIT*.

EDD Online users do not have to know these tags, but they should be aware
of Wright's source classification involved, because Wright may have given
them different grades of credit (cf. Markus 2019b on the *Supplement*). The
corresponding three sub-filters of the filter *sources* are included in Figure 6.19.

The titles in Figure 6.19 have been edited by us. Perhaps surprisingly, some
of the short titles (or names) have dates of publication, others do not. The
reason is that some of the names stand for several works and some of the titles
for several editions. The smart tag, in any case, clarifies matters.

---

[7] As a result of this highlighting, the background is temporarily faded.

Most users may prefer to make use of these selected lists, which comprise about a tenth or less of the whole, as a helpful offer to retrieve dialectal secondary titles, on the one hand, and 'literature', on the other hand. However, some authors, such as Burns, Hardy and Sir Walter Scott, really belong to both groups. This is why we have provided a comprehensive list (in the order of Figure 6.19 the third one), which does not merge the two aforementioned lists, but only joins them: first the seemingly endless list of so-called dialect literature, followed by the shorter one of literary authors and titles. It is thus guaranteed that, for example, Burns, which we have in the *literary* list, whereas Wright has him in the *dialectal* list, is still found when users search for him in the *complete* list.

We decided to offer this option of the combined list called *dial. + lit. (complete)* in view of the enormous amount and complexity of Wright's references to sources. The relative inaccessibility of this *complete* list is also because it includes a large amount of expository and documentary texts: journals and gazettes, chronicles, accounts, surveys, guides, reports, essays, letters, parish and monasterial registers, court protocols and so on – partly genres that reflect the real language of people more authentically than literary works and the familiar descriptive language books (such as grammars and dictionaries). We edited these references of list 4 as best we could, but it proved impossible for us to trace and verify all of them bibliographically, due to Wright's often fragmentary identification of them and due to the amount of work undertaken for correction and completion. To the extent that we have been able to identify the abbreviations, however, we have always endowed the short titles of the lists with a smart tag mechanism. Users here again have the option of opening a window with the full title of the given source – just click on its abbreviated author and/or title in our lists. These full references had to be kept in the background in favour of the short titles because the long titles would have clogged the screen and the short titles are the very ones that Wright had used in the entries. In the reference lists, we only risked minor changes, for example, in the form of first names added.

While such expository and documentary sources are, then, less easily accessible, both in the case of the *EDD* and in general, they have lately become, and should be in the case of the *EDD*, a most promising field of linguistic study, particularly in view of LModE. Users are invited to browse in the sub-menu of the extremely comprehensive combined list, perhaps in the attempt to trace unknown authors or titles. If they wish to check whether a certain source has at all been used by the *EDD*, this is where to look it up.

As mentioned, the smart-tag information on the full titles behind the short ones has also been implemented for all the titles of the complete list, but, unlike the selections, the keywords on this complete list were not regularised

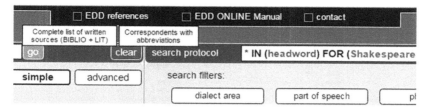

Figure 6.20 Interface option 'EDD references'

or normalised. They were edited up to a point, but the titles here essentially come in the shape of the first abbreviation used in the *EDD*.

Our reluctance to re-edit every single title of Wright's sources is due to the enormous quantity of the sources and Wright's lack of consistency in using abbreviations for them. Above all, we were confronted with a large number of gaps and errors in the bibliography. The point of quantity can be concluded from the length of the *EDD* bibliography in its book form: 50 pages, in small print with two columns on each page. In our Excel table of this bibliography (see below), 4,879 titles have been counted, many of them with a dozen or more abbreviations attributed to them.

The Excel table of the *complete* list can be triggered in the top headline of our interface (called '*EDD* references') (see the left option in Figure 6.20).

When opened, the *Complete list* provides all abbreviations used in the *EDD* and again reveals which titles and how many we have corrected, complemented or inserted (in blue). Users also can copy complete titles from this Excel table. Figure 6.21, popping up with a click on the left option, is an extract of the table.

The table may suggest the kind of problems with which my team and I were confronted concerning the identification of sources. Title 59, for example, refers to the name of the author of the *Terrae Filius*. The name is spelt with an *e* in the abbreviation (*Amherst*), but with a *u* in the title's full version (*Amhurst*). Lines 69 ff. are concerned with three different authors/editors by the name of Anderson, which can be a problem if the short titles omit the first names. Moreover, Wright obviously used different editions of the ballads edited by R. Anderson, but exactly which edition is meant in a given context is impossible for the computer to decide – we mainly took the publication dates as a basis of decision. Line 61 provides quite a number of abbreviations, some of them with spelling variation, and may, thus, give us an idea of the difficulty to refer these abbreviations to the titles of Wright's references.

By the use of the blue colour (in the case of this book's grayscale figures, in light grey), the table reveals which titles and how many we have corrected, complemented or inserted.

	A	B	F
58	Chs.	Altrincham and Bowdon Guardian. (1895-1896)	Altrinch. Guard.;Altrincham Guard.;Altrincham Guardian;Altrincham and Bowdon Guardian;Bow St. Police Case
59	Oxf.	Amhurst, Nicholas.— Terræ Filius; or, the Secret History of the University of Oxford. R. Francklin: London, 1726. (also written Amherst)	Amherst Terrae Fil.
60	Cum.	Anderson, R.—Ballads in the Cumberland dialect: with notes and a glossary. 8vo, Carlisle, 1805.	Anderson Ballads;Anderson Poet. Wks.
61	Cum.	Anderson, R.—Ballads in the Cumberland dialect, chiefly by R. Anderson, with notes and a glossary; the remainder by various authors, several of which have been never before published. 12mo, Wigton, 1808 [and var. ed.].	Anderson Ballads;Anderson Poet. Wks.;Anderson Ballads The Aunty;Wully Miller;Anderson Codbeck Wed.;Anderson Clay Daubin';Anderson Clay Daubin;Anderson Buck o' Kingwatter;Anderson Adveyce to Nanny;Anderson Heddersgill Keatie;Anderson Tom Linton;Anderson The Cram;Anderson Cram;Clay Daubin;Cocker o' Codbeck;Codbeck Weddin;Dedication;Jeff and Job;Nichol the Newsmonger;Nicol the Newsmonger;Redbreest;The Aunty;Tom Linton;Uncle Wully;Worton Wedding
62	Abd.	Anderson, William.—The Piper of Peebles, a Tale. By the Lamb-leader. T. Colvill, 1794	Anderson Piper of Peebles;Anderson Piper o' Peebles
63	Lin.	Anderson, Charles H. J.—The Lincoln Pocket-guide. 12mo, Lincoln, 1874.	Anderson Pocket Guide;Anderson Lin. Pocket Guide;Lin. Pocket Guide
64	Sc.	Anderson, David.—Poems chiefly in the Scottish dialect, and ed., 8vo, Aberdeen, 1826.	Anderson Poems;Sanderson Essay
65	Abd.	Anderson, William.—Rhymes, Reveries, and Reminiscences. 12mo, Aberdeen, 1851 [and ed. 1867].	Anderson Rhymes;Anderson ib.{{Rhymes}}
66	Midl.	Anderton, Thomas. Letters from a Country House. Simpkin, Marshall &Co: London, 1891.	Anderton Lett.;Anderton Lett. Cy. House;Anderton Lett. from Cy. House
67	Lin.	Andrew, William. The History of Winterton and the Adjoining Villages, in the Northern Division of Manley, in the County of Lincoln; With a Notice of Their Antiquities. A.D. English: Hull, 1836.	Andrew Hist. Winterton
68	Sc.	Andrews, William.—Bygone Church Life in Scotland. Ed. by William Andrews. 8vo. London. 1899.	Andrews Bygone Ch. Life;Andrews Ch. Life;Sc. Parl. Act

Figure 6.21 Extract of Excel table of printed sources (dialects, titles and abbreviations)

The source data that refer to 'correspondents' (*unprinted* sources), are likewise presented in the top headline of our interface (see Figure 6.20). The correspondents are given throughout the *Dictionary* by their initials. In our interface we have abstained from listing them in this way (unless we could not find the full name) since hardly any of the initials will be familiar to users. Instead, we have generally given the 'correspondents' their full names. If users wish they can trace the number of females or clergymen in this group, or – more likely – the county-affiliation of the contributors. On the other hand, users interested in the relation between the abbreviations and the full names of correspondents may consult the survey provided in the Excel table, to be activated in the headline button *EDD references*.

The role of unprinted sources (including 'slips' sent by correspondents) will now also be subject to possible analyses based on quantification, in the same way that the dialectal and literary contributors can be quantified. This quanti-fication can be achieved by special modes of the sorting routine in the white box at the top of the entry window (as mentioned earlier). Here different columns of the findings can be isolated, alphabetised and counted.

If users wish to identify correspondents that we have not been able to trace based on the given initials, they are invited to do so with the help of the final option added after the list of abbreviations, *UNIDENTIFIED*. The retrieval list provided after the activation of the button for these non-identified initials comprises no less than 2,158 headwords. This high number reveals that Wright and his team were negligent in unequivocally identifying the names of their helpers.[8] The *column 2 counted* mode allows for future users to see at first glance which of the unidentified initials are the most frequently repeated ones. These are particularly suitable to encourage further endeavours to correlate the initials with full names.

Psychologically, the inconsistencies in the *EDD*'s references to one and the same title are entirely comprehensible and can readily be apologised. For the retrieval by the computer, however, the use or absence of a hyphen or apostrophe is fatal. While the sources on this basis of inconsistent spelling were occasionally difficult for us to trace, the worse cases were those when abbreviations did not have any referent in the bibliography at all, or when, *vice versa*, a given title of Wright's bibliography could not be correlated with the abbreviations used for sources. On the basis of publication dates and other contextual hints, we filled such bibliographical gaps as best we could, supported in this task by scholarly bibliographies and by Google. The rudimentary character of some of the references to sources may be illustrated by the abbreviation '19th Cent.'. Only after some philological work could we decide that this most probably is a reference to the short-lived periodical *The Nineteenth Century* (C. Kegan Paul and Co.: London, 1887–1900). As mentioned, we marked all such – sometimes hypothetical – additions and untraceable abbreviations by blue colour. While they were assimilated by us to some kind of stylesheet, the editorial mode of the titles taken over by us from Wright's long original reference list was left unchanged.

The smart-tag window opened in Figure 6.19 for presenting the full title behind an abbreviation is triggered by a simple click on that abbreviation. As mentioned, it works for the first three of the sub-filters of the sources (i.e. the written-source documents). The correspondents (in the sub-filter *unprinted*) did not need this gadget, because their full names, normally given, stand for themselves. Only in a small number of cases could we not identify the person behind initials.[9]

Our editorial work has not only made the *EDD* bibliography more comprehensive and more transparent than the one of the book version but has also brought to light the enormous share of second-hand references in the *EDD*.

---

[8] The three-letter initials for correspondents, for example, occasionally refer to different names and people alike.

[9] For example, 'A.C.' ambiguously stands for either 'Miss A. Carter' or 'A. Clear'.

The best example for this is probably the ubiquitous use of John Jamieson's *Etymological Dictionary of the Scottish Language* (1808). It stands to reason that Wright and his team used county-specific sources for England and, in particular, its north (where they lived) much more than for Scotland, Ireland and Wales, for which the data is often based on more general reference books. This uneven use of references to counties and regions has been noticed before (Praxmarer 2010). However, to what extent this lack of balance was precisely the case and what the repercussions are in view of the validity of the data, can now be studied on a more empirical basis than in the past. It is also worth repeating here (cf. Section 6.3.2) that our cheropleth maps are based on normalised figures of occurrence (of types), with the absolute figures related to the sum totals of occurrences. The fact that Wright had areal 'favourites' is, thus, levelled out.

To sum up this section on the *EDD* sources, users find four elaborated options: (1) a list of selected names of authors and/or works of specific literature on dialect (*dialectal*); (2) a list of selected names and titles referring to literary, that is, fictional and poetic works (*literary*); (3) a combined and complete reference list of all written sources (*dial. + lit. complete*) and finally (4) a complete list of the full names of various contributors (*unprinted*). Once again, lists (1) and (2) are extremely selective. Why this separation of two short reference lists from a long and complete one? The answer is that lists (1) and (2), due to their moderate length and our editorial improvement, encourage specific author queries and also combined queries, for example, a search for all selected authors at a time. Lists (3) and (4) have also been edited by us up to a point, but still have deficits in that the titles and names are partly incomplete, ambiguous and inconsistent, particularly in the use of abbreviations.

6.3.6   Phonetic

Wright's phonetic transcription is very similar to the IPA transcription (International Phonetic Association), which was to become standard in the twentieth century and has widely been part of the curriculum in our universities, the main difference being that word accent is marked in the *EDD* by a high dot after the stressed syllable of a word, rather than by a high stroke before it. For the rest, users meet with a few unfamiliar symbols of transcription as well as diacritics which can all be produced with the help of the special keyboard, available when one clicks on the filter *phonetic*.

The order of the special characters and diacritics on this keyboard is self-made but simple, ranging from the vowel *a* and its 'derivatives' (such as the ash-ligature) to the variants of the other vowels, that is, of *e*, *i*, *o* and *u*, and, in a final line, providing variants of consonants and diacritics, such as the raised dot. The lists also include Scandinavian graphemes (such as <ø>), (German)

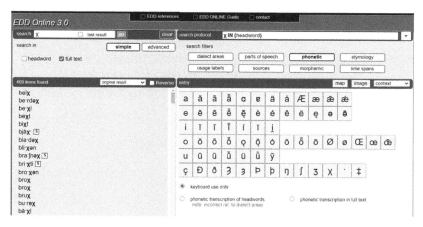

Figure 6.22 Search for χ (velar fricative) in *full text*

umlaut graphemes (e.g. <ö>) and historical symbols that have not come down to us in the inventory of the IPA, such as the thorn (þ).

Occasional transcriptions that are not in the 'head'-part of the entries, that is, not in their first paragraphs, but rather in the citations, originating from Wright's dialectological precursors, have likewise been included in the set of characters and diacritics – here some tentative practises of narrow transcription and characters of pseudo-phonetic spellings have to be expected.

This selective keyboard (see Figure 6.22) is meant to be used for the production of special characters in whatever context, that is, also in contexts outside the search for phonetic transcriptions referring to headwords or the full text. Users may, for example, be interested in the survival of ash-ligatures (æ) or of yoghs (ȝ, ȝ), be it in variants or quotations. Figure 6.22 demonstrates this default mode of *keyboard use only* by tracing the old velar fricative χ in the *simple* search mode *full text* (see the button above the retrieval list).

Note that the query of Figure 6.22 targets all occurrences of χ regardless of their context and of the meaning of this character, and that this query is, therefore, not identical to the search for the same symbol as a *phonetic transcription* in *full text* (for which see the button in the right half of the interface). The former query includes, for example, the occasional use of the letter chi (χ) in Greek words.

The latter query (within phonetic transcriptions) is illustrated in Figure 6.23.

The quantity of matches in Figure 6.23 is a bit less than in the case of Figure 6.22, because now, as a subset of the dictionary's text, only the

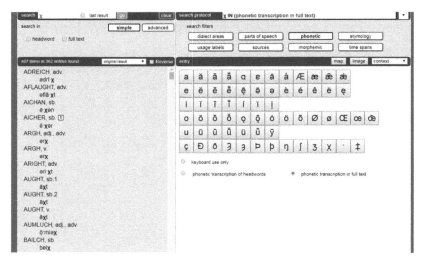

Figure 6.23 Search for [χ] (velar fricative) as a symbol of *phonetic transcription* in the filter option *full text* (right half of interface)

phonetic transcriptions clearly marked as such by square brackets have been eligible for the query. Unlike in Figure 6.22, the phonetic findings have been subordinated to the headwords they belong to. This is in line with the default presentation mode *original result*. Users can also opt for the sorting mode *column 2 counted*, which lists and counts the phonetic strings containing χ without additionally presenting the headwords to which they belong.

Figures 6.22 and 6.23 reveal that the combination of phonetic *full text* queries with filters is blocked in both cases – see the red frames. While the *last result* mode offers itself for by-passing this restriction, the output of such combined queries, in particular, of queries including dialect areas, is non-reliable and has to be checked manually because phonetic transcriptions and dialect markers are not systematically linked. Accordingly, the mapping of quantitative results of phonetic queries should be handled with care or should altogether be avoided. An illustration of this trap will be provided in Section 8.3.3 by means of case studies.

6.3.7   Morphemic

This filter permits the opening of options from a limited list of common bound suffixes and prefixes, such as *-ing* and *be-* respectively. Since word compositions with at least one bound lexical morpheme are, by definition, derivations, the morphemic query automatically refers, on the one hand, to the parameter of *derivations* (in the *expanded* mode). On the other hand, entries themselves are occasionally derivations so that headwords are also automatically included in this query. In other words, *morphemic* is simply a button for users to simplify the handling of *EDD Online*. One selects a prefix or suffix, which is then automatically copied into the query box and applied on both headwords and derivations. Needless to say that users may also search for bound morphemes of their own choice which are not listed in our *morphemic* selection. But then they have to search twice: once for *headwords* and then for *derivations*.

The selective affix lists of the *morphemic* filter have been limited to non-grammatical morphemes, relevant to word formation. Grammatical morphemes, such as third person singular -*s*, have been excluded from the lists because they could only be retrieved from a parsed corpus. The filter *usage labels*, in its sub-menu *syntax*, however, provides quite a number of grammatical/syntactic features as query keywords (see Section 6.3.3).

The following example illustrating the morphemic filter provides all strings ending on *able* – 192 items. As Figure 6.24 shows (in the protocol and in the list of retrieved words), the query is automatically applied to headwords and derivations.[10]

While the retrieval list of Figure 6.24 has produced occasional misfits, such as CABLE, the combination of derivations and headwords in one retrieval list is clearly an advantage because users are not confronted with two separate lists which would have to be merged and alphabetised before they could be analysed.

6.3.8   Etymology

As Wright was also a very competent historical linguist,[11] the *EDD*, in the 'comments' of the entries, keeps referring to etymological roots. The etymology filter not only often provides the main earlier languages that Late Modern English dialect is based on, such as Old English and Norwegian, but allows access to many cognates, such as from Gothic and Low German (on the quality of etymological information in the *EDD*, cf. Chamson 2010 and 2012). In a query, the filter provides the languages searched for, the etyma/words of these languages and, as usual, the headwords involved. Figure 6.25 shows the 185 matches of a query searching for Dutch etymologies and filtered by all

---

[10] Unlike derivations, headwords are capitalised.
[11] He authored or co-authored several historical grammars, such as *An Elementary Middle English Grammar* (Joseph Wright and [his wife] Elizabeth Mary Wright) 1923 (2nd ed., London: Oxford University Press, 1928).

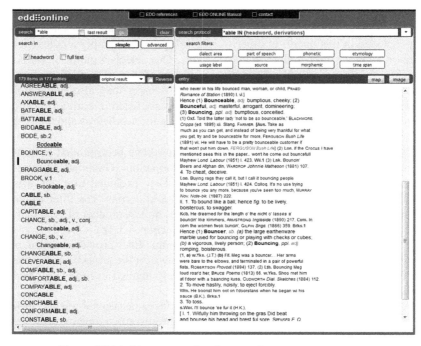

Figure 6.24 *able* as a morphemic query item

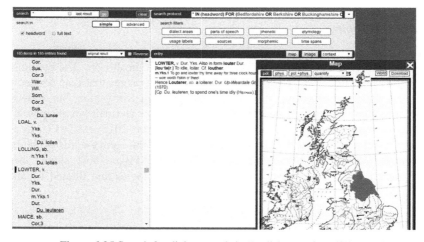

Figure 6.25 Search for dialect words in English counties affiliated with Dutch etymology, plus distribution map of a selected headword concerned with regard to counties

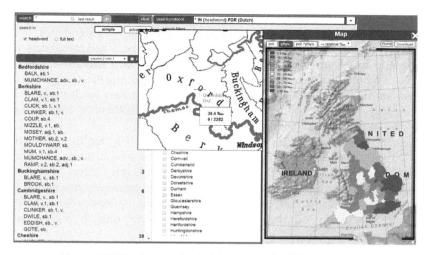

Figure 6.26 Dutch etymological impact on English county dialects (*column 2 with 1*)

county dialects of England. The map reveals at a glimpse in which particular counties of England the etymon that I selected (Dutch *leuteren*) played a role.

The logic of the map creation is that **all** dialectal areas of an entry, whether counties, regions or nations, and whether from England or any other country, including those overseas, are highlighted on the map if the user clicks on the entry, i.e. in the case of Figure 6.25 on LOWTHER. If areas outside the UK are concerned, a world map pops up, instead of the map of the British Isles. As mentioned earlier, there are also two alternative options of maps in addition to the 'political' (i.e. outline) map, namely a physical map and a hybrid one. Moreover, there is the option of creating synoptic maps – by first counting the areal references (in the *column 2* modes of the sorting box[12]) and then transferring the multi-entry quantities to the *quantify* map (see Section 6.3.2). Whichever option is preferred, one can always click on an areal abbreviation, for example, Yks., to see on the map what the abbreviation stands for, where the area concerned is, and what its share in a given query result is.

Figure 6.26 probatively illustrates the distribution of headwords with a Dutch etymological background in English counties, this time on a physical map.

As one would expect, the Dutch influence turns out to be remarkably strong in Sussex/Kent, East Anglia and Durham, and strikingly weak within the

---

[12] Either *column 2 with 1* or *column 2 counted*.

triangle London – Oxford – Cambridge. East Anglia and Durham were among the areas in England where the growing cloth industry played a significant role from the late Middle Ages up to the nineteenth century,[13] and this industry implies trading contacts with the Dutch and Flemish. Kent and Sussex were likely to profit from such contacts due to their being geographical neighbours of the Netherlands.[14] On the other hand, the said triangle may be characterised by a relative social and cultural autonomy so that the distribution concerning this area in Figure 6.26 makes sense.

Searching for etymologically relevant languages is only the first optional mode of retrieval within the etymological filter. The second mode allows a search for specific etyma, including possibly morphemic strings and also graphemes, such as $<æ>$ and $<ʒ>$, with both strings and languages provided. With the help of the sorting routine, the findings can optionally be ordered language-specifically so that, for example, all Old English etyma are listed together.

The strings searched for have to be typed into the general query box. Figure 6.27 illustrates this option by showing an extract of the screen.

Users may combine the two types of etymological queries with other filters, such as the dialect sub-filters. These would, thus, also permit finding the etymological (e.g. Scandinavian) background of, say, Yorkshire or Northumbrian words. In this case the dialect filter would be focused on the area of interest and the etymological filter would have to be set on *select all (languages)*. One has to consider, however, that Wright has not commented on the etymological background of every dialect word in the *EDD*. Cognates are a special extra, not reliably and consistently provided in the *EDD*. Quantifications of etymological findings, therefore, have to be interpreted with care.

6.3.9   Time Spans

The *EDD* does not provide any direct information on the time of usage of a certain form or word, but only the dates of the sources referred to in the given context. Of course, this only holds true for the written sources. Our pool of dates is also limited in that it only contains years – months and other more precise pieces of temporal information were ignored when we tagged our XML-text. Circumscriptive time references, however, of the type 'in the first

---

[13] Cf. the map in *Historical Atlas of Britain* 1981: 190.
[14] The close connection of Norfolk with cloth industry and the trading contacts with the Netherlands forms the background to the letters of the Paston family, see *Illustrated Letters of the Paston Family*. 1989: 12–15.

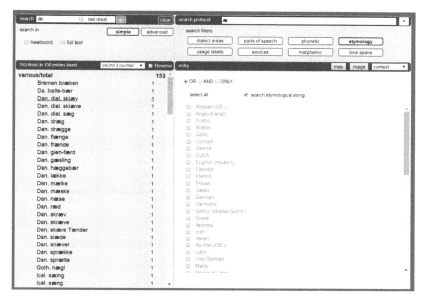

Figure 6.27 Words with ash-ligature arranged language-wise in the *column 2 counted* mode (filter *etymology*)

quarter of the 19th century', have been interpreted/normalised by us in that they were transformed into clear numbers of years or of spans of years.

Users can activate either of two modes: *time span* or (exact) *year* (see Figure 6.28).

In the first mode on the left of Figure 6.28, users may fill in spans of time they are interested in, such as 1150 to 1500, and thus produce a list of the headwords whose time of occurrence, i.e. whose phase of publication dates, overlaps with the tackled time span 1150 to 1500. In concrete terms, this means that the earliest and the latest years found in the entries may lie outside the defined query time as long as there is an overlap. The logic of this time-span query is that the string that users are looking for was known at some stage of the time span given in the left query box of Figure 6.28, in our case, Middle English. The use of this mode 1 is illustrated in Figure 6.29, now with the time span of 1500 to 1700 (Early Modern English).

The headword ABRICOCK is associated in its citations with two Early Modern English dates, 1548 and 1636. These two dates, then, mark the time span valid for this entry, defined in the headers of our XML entry text. My query asked for the time from 1500 to 1700. Accordingly, due to the temporal overlap, ABRICOCK is rightly included.

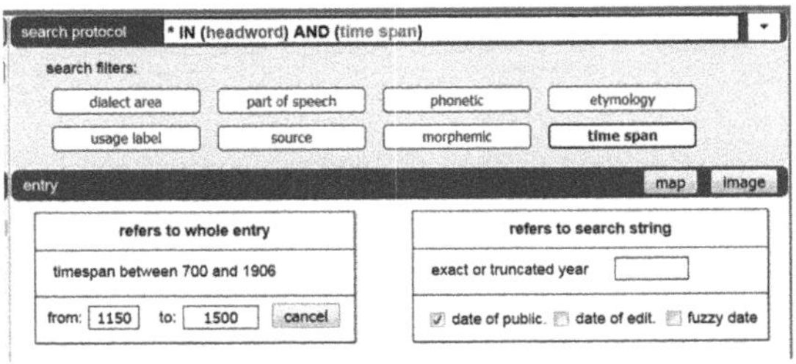

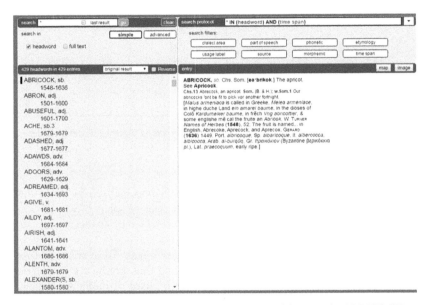

Figure 6.28 The two modes of time reference

Figure 6.29 Search for *time span* (mode 1), with example ABRICOCK opened

Mode 1, it may be added, should be used with care because it implies high-frequency retrievals. For example, users should avoid unrestricted nineteenth-century queries, with * as the search string, because such queries would start producing results the size of which are hardly manageable by both the computer and the users. But mode 1 offers itself for complex combinations of query items. For example, we may search for *a** in *variants,* focussing on Yorkshire. This is probably narrow enough a query to allow for leaving the time span unspecified, for example by typing in 700 to 1904. The result list (319 variants) nicely demonstrates the role of *h*-dropping in Yorkshire, for example, concerning the headword HACKER, with its variant *accer* added, plus the county concerned (e.Yks.) and the time of occurrence (or at least of the publication of the sources), 1790 to 1898. The time factor reflects the prominent role of *h*-dropping in the nineteenth century (cf. Markus 2002).

The second mode (see again Figure 6.28, right-hand side) is meant for temporal close-up studies. If users type in, for example, the year number '1840', only exact hits are retrieved. The pinning down of dialect data to a single year at first sight may not seem sensible, but it could be of interest, for example, to users focusing on the last years covered by Wright, 1900 to 1905. Truncation is possible here: '190*' means '1900' to '1904' (there is no later year). The main advantage of this second mode is that the numbers of year precisely refer to whichever type of word formation (compounds, derivations, etc.) has been opted for, whereas mode (1) globally refers to entries as a whole. The reason for this difference is that we developed an algorithm for each entry as a whole based on the years given. When these range from, say, 1850 to 1900, with only three years mentioned (1850, 1879 and 1900), a query exactly for the year 1855 (our mode 2) would produce nil results, but the range query along the lines of our mode 1 would produce valid matches. But – to underline this by repetition – they necessarily, and in some cases inaccurately, refer to the entry as a whole so that they are of limited value for *advanced* search modes.

On this occasion, we should remember that the connection between dates and lexical units is generally a rather indirect one in the *EDD*. Dates do not refer to word forms, but to the sources of literature selected mainly for reasons of illustration. Moreover, we cannot rely on the earliest dates given in an entry always to represent exact dates of the first occurrence. Unlike the compilers of the *Oxford English Dictionary (OED)*, which, started in 1857 and by the 1890s was surely prestigious enough to be a good candidate for serving as a model, Wright had obviously no ambition of compiling a primarily historical diction-ary, not even for the claimed period from 1700 to 1904. Historical precision can even less be expected since dialect lexis is usually long-lived and, due to its mostly spoken basis, hard to date.

Nevertheless, *EDD Online* can boast of providing some valid connection to time by reference to the dates of sources. In our programming work, we have correlated time (when searched for in terms of special years) with both dialectal forms and meanings, always with the caveat in mind that the histor-ical picture thus presented may be somewhat blurred in individual cases. By and large, however, the great many sources that Wright has used, particularly if dates of editions are excluded in the time parameter (see the next paragraph), may be representative enough of the fixation of data on the timeline.

The exclusion of dates of editions and of fuzzy dates is triggered by the de-activation of the buttons on offer underneath the field for marking the year number. By default, all three buttons are activated. The button *fuzzy date* provides year numbers in the retrieval window marked by brackets. This means that these numbers are rough-and-ready calculations implemented by us and based on 1900 as the temporal zero point. We, thus, translated '20 years ago' into '[1880]', '20 or 25 years ago' into '[1875–1880]', 'the last century' into '[1701–1800]', etc. In cases where a temporal phrase of this kind was not Wright's own, but a quotation from one of Wright's sources, we took the publication date of that source as the temporal zero point, which meant manual work. Given that Wright has often quoted second-hand, for example, from Jamieson (1808), with a large number of undated primary sources involved, we were aware of a certain inaccuracy in our temporal interpretations. It was simply impossible for us to trace back the publication dates of all sources to their origins. And the origin of folklore culture and language is often undatable *per se*. To counter critical comments on this point, I would like to add that, by and large, the fuzzy dates play a quantitatively negligible role in the *EDD*. For the year 1870, for example, the search engine produces only fourteen head-word matches of fuzzy dates versus 1,716 matches of precise dates and 113 dates of year for editions.

7   Retrieval Window (Advanced Mode)

7.1   General Mode of Entry Presentation, Highlighting and Use of Colour

The entries concerned by whatever query are by default presented on the interface in a text mode based on our deciphering, editing and correction of the original text. In the retrieval window (left half of the interface), the entry headwords are always automatically added (in capital letters) except for *full text* queries. The strings of the query are subordinated to the headwords and appear in boldface. The selected element is marked by a vertical stroke left of it. In the entry window (on the right), the elements searched for are highlighted. Here the main units of the entry come in different colours: the headwords in black (they are capitalised again), the parts of speech in red, the dialects in brown and so on. The text is presented without the original linebreaking of words by hyphens and without other layout details that are liable to 'confuse' the computer, but with the (frequent) complemented units of complex lexemes abbreviated in the original by hyphens (and now marked by a light grey), moreover with the (rare) necessary emendations.

An alternative mode of presentation is that of the original images of the *EDD* entries reproduced from the paper version, i.e. in black and white (click on *image*). Users can, thus, always check the correctness of our editing, as we could during our work. Figure 7.1 shows the image for PENT-HOUSE, one of the fifty-three findings in a query for *house*.

As shown in Figure 7.1, the searched string is highlighted not only in the entry window but also in the image window. This also holds true for other search items than headwords, for example, *full text*, and was achieved by the addition of position coordinates to each single 'value' (mostly words) in our XML version of the *EDD*. This addition of coordinates turned out to be rather labour-intensive, but I trust that users will appreciate the entry images to be easily accessibility.

Figure 7.1 is based on a query within the *simple* mode (*headwords*), which is what this book has, in fact, so far focused on, holding back the complexity of the 'advanced' parameters. Boldfacing, colours, highlighting and all the other

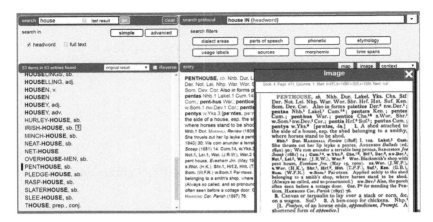

Figure 7.1 PENTHOUSE as one of the matches of search for *house* as *headword* (plus image)

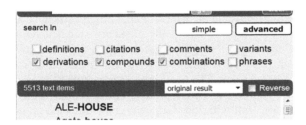

Figure 7.2 Sub-menu of the *advanced* mode of searches

items of website design are, however, always the same, no matter what queries and filters refer to. In the remainder of this chapter, we discuss the different parameters available beyond headwords in detail.

7.2   Survey: Retrieval Window

Mention has been made of *phrases* and various types of word formation, such as *compounds* and *derivations*, as query objects. All these play an important quantitative role in the *EDD*, but they are somewhat 'hidden' within entries, unlike in most modern dictionaries where many of these types are lemmatised. To access them in *EDD Online*, users of the interface simply click on the *advanced* button (top left). The sub-menu of this button is shown in Figure 7.2.

As one can see in Figure 7.2, the *advanced* mode opens access to eight parameters. Before we discuss them in detail, the issue of the compatibility of

Figure 7.3 Marking acceptable and unacceptable combinations of parameters and filters

different parameters should be raised, and, moreover, the question of which filters can be combined with them. We thought that users would wish some help on these points. The information is given by the red frames surrounding unacceptable buttons. Figure 7.3 (in colour) demonstrates the principle.

Figure 7.3 demonstrates that the search for *compounds* could also be run as part of a combined query including *derivations* and *combinations*, but excludes pairings with *definitions*, *citations*, *variants* and *phrases*. While the inclusion of *phrases* would have made sense from the philological point of view and was, therefore, seriously considered, we finally opted against it because the structure of phrases proved incompatible with the XQuery routine applied for *compounds* (as well as *derivations* and *combinations*). As to the filters, only four of them can combine with *compounds*.

For further details and a summary of these rules of compatibility, see Section 7.11.

7.3   Definitions

The first parameter of the *advanced* mode, *definitions*, restricts a query to those sections of entries that topicalise the meaning of words. These sections, however, are not as 'purely' semantic as may be expected. They comprise sources and, occasionally, their dates of publication. To keep semantic information apart from such distracting items, which can be retrieved using specific filter buttons, we have excluded sources and dates in our tagging and the query policy concerning semantics.

The search option *definitions* offers itself as a basis for word-field studies. For example, users may search for *girl*, at the same time activating the

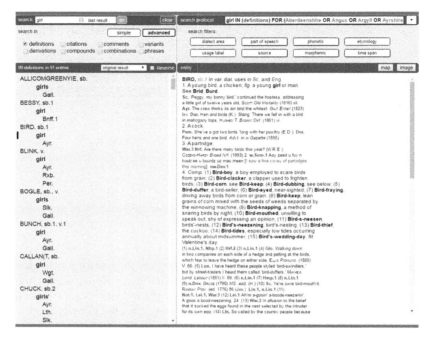

Figure 7.4 Search for *girl* (implicitly truncated) as a string of definition, plus filter *dialect area* = all Scottish counties

dialect-button (e.g. for Scottish counties). They will then get 99 strings of *girl(s)* in the *definitions* block plus the dialects attributed to them (see Figure 7.4).

The dialect words themselves, for example WENCH, have to be checked individually because their syntax in relation to the dialects has proved to be somewhat erratic. In other words, not each string in a defining part of an entry is semantically significant for the headword of that entry. The dialect words themselves can also be conveniently isolated with the *last result* mode (discussed in Section 6.2.2). In the present case, this mode would have the advantage of allowing for an arrangement of the 48 'girl-words', most of them synonyms, in alphabetical order, with the dialect areas subordinated (in the *original result* mode). Alternatively, users may subordinate the dialect words to the individual counties (in *column 2 with 1* mode). This mode is illustrated in Figure 7.5.

The highlighted sample of Figure 7.5 also demonstrates the problem, addressed earlier, of the somewhat unreliable syntax of entries in view of semantic queries. The headword STUNK does not directly refer to [girl], but

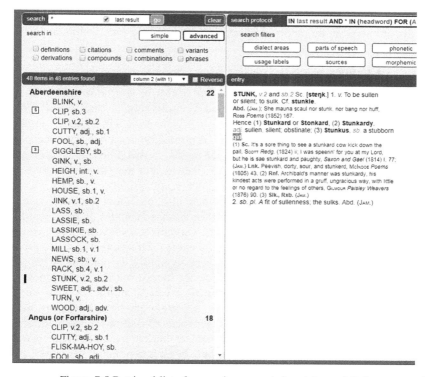

Figure 7.5 Retrieval list after previous search for *girl* as a defining term and after a subsequent *last-result* retrieval, in the *column 2 with 1* presentation mode

only in the derivation *stunku*s 'a stubborn girl'. By and large, however, this lack of referential precision is rather the exception than the rule because the dialect words defined in entries are mostly the headwords, as nearly in all cases seen in Figure 7.5.[1]

As regards any of the filters, they can be added within the general limits, in this case with *dialect areas*, *usage labels, sources* and *etymology*. It has, however, to be emphasised that with long entries, the attribution of such filter terms to defining strings may lead us astray in a few cases due to the occasional extreme complexity of the entry structure. In other words, users should check

---

[1] One of the counter-examples is CLYTE, where the defining term *girl* refers to a compound given under CLYTE, *Clytie-lass*. Since CLYTE means a 'mass of any liquid ... material', the sememe [girl] can obviously be traced in the second element of the compound, *-lass,* rather than in the first element *Clytie*.

with semantic queries of this kind whether the defining term really refers to the headword given in the retrieval window or some sub-lexeme within an entry.

7.4   Citations

The button *citations* implies the search for strings of text quoted by Wright from sources, including unprinted information contributed by 'correspondents'. Users would, of course, also be interested in all these sources themselves, as well as their dialects and, if printed, their dates of publication. This presumed interest urged us to reflect the possibilities of combining searches for citation text with those for dialects and the features addressed by our other filters.

In the blocks of citations, Wright often also provides volumes, pages, paragraphs and, in many cases, first- and second-hand sources. In other words, these paragraphs confront us with data of a very mixed nature. By their syntax they are the most unpredictable part of the entries. This comes as no surprise because the 'style sheet' of the text in these sections only partly depends on Wright's own editorial work, but mostly on the diverse authors he has quoted. Naturally, the output is bound to be formally inconsistent, the more so when several of our filter types (*dialects, labels, etymology* and *time span*) come into play in a given query. What also makes the blocks of citations problematic and anything but a homogeneous 'corpus' is the fact that some parts in them are not quotations from dialect sources at all, but, in fact, comments verbalised by Wright's linguistic predecessors or non-professional contemporaries. Some of the quotations have an expository and defining rather than an illustrating function. The heterogeneity of the 'citations' is increased by the fact that the degree of dialectal language in the quoted texts, both in pronunciation and spelling, varies from dialect to dialect and from author to author. By and large, however, the *EDD* quotations serve the purpose of demonstrating the point made in an entry's preceding paragraph, which often verbalises meaning rather than a special dialectal form.

Owing to these various factors in the *citations*, we temporarily considered disallowing the combination of citation queries with nearly all filters. However, we finally decided not to be too restrictive, instead encouraging users to select data of their own choice and at their own risk. To provide an example of this semi-reliable type of query, we could select (Scottish) *au*-spelling in texts quoted from Robert Burns (Figure 7.6).

Figure 7.6 shows that the attribution of the *au*-spelling in *Auld* to a work by Burns is correct in this case. But there are, admittedly, a few counter-examples in the 359 matches retrieved in the query given in Figure 7.6. Results from combined citation queries, therefore, should be interpreted with care and checked against individual entry contexts. In spite of this weakness, the

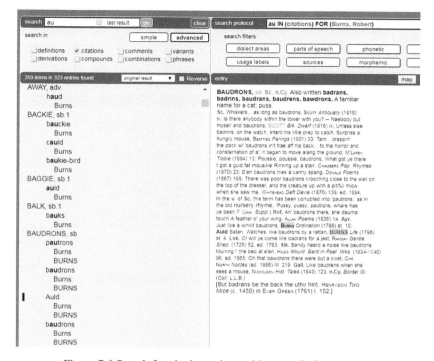

Figure 7.6 Search for citation strings with <au> in Burns texts

retrieval lists of citation queries of the type of Figure 7.6 allow for the usual sorting facilities, thus providing an optional survey of the various words with *au*-spelling, or, if several authors have been selected, of the relative role of each of these authors.

To increase its versatile use, the parameter of *citations* also harbours a rudimentary kwic-concordance, with the presentation of four strings to the left and four strings to the right of the keyword. The first and the second slot to either side can be used for an alphabetised re-arrangement. The concordance can be activated with a click on *citations* and another click on *with concordance* in the ensuing pop-up window. The default mode, however, is *without concordance* because the creation of the concordance takes some extra time for calculation.

Figure 7.7 demonstrates the functioning of the parameter of *citations,* with *wife* as a search string and the *concordance* mode activated.

We have also considered the possibility of optionally presenting the full quotations. But given their inadequacy as part of a proper 'corpus', i.e. given

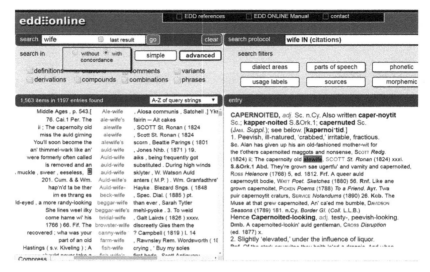

Figure 7.7 Search for *wife* (truncated) as a string of citations, with kwic-concordance (extract)

their mixed structure mentioned earlier, we have finally dropped this idea. The concordance is certainly the better tool for exploiting the quotations. The 1,563 matches of the query for *wife*, ranging from *ale-wife* to *witch-wife*, may raise our interest about typical patterns of compounding. The options of the alphabetisation of defined columns is a most helpful tool for studying collocations. These options can be selected in the white sorting box at the top of the retrieval window. The alphabetisation is demonstrated in Figure 7.8.

Figure 7.8 shows that the phrase *the good wife* is significantly frequent, which attests to its idiomatic quality. By the same token, the concordance mode encourages queries concerning formal variation. The phrase *good wife*, for example, also frequently appears in the form *gude/guid wife* and as a compound *guidwife/guid-wife*.

7.5   Comments

One of the query sections or parameters in *EDD Online* is that of *comments*. These are bracketed sections of the entries that are clearly of secondary relevance. We distinguished two different main types of comments: those within a block of citations, with a normalising or explanatory function concerning passages in broad dialect (as it were, subtitles of difficult dialectal

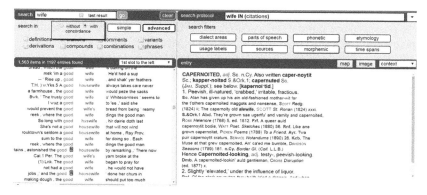

Figure 7.8 Kwik concordance of *wife* as keyword in the *citations* parameter, with left-side collocates (first slot)

text); and comments at the end of the block of citations, which have clearly larger fonts than the text of the preceding quotation blocks.

From the point of view of dialectology, the comments are of secondary importance. It is true that they occasionally refer to dialects, particularly to American and other overseas Englishes. For the rest, they often topicalise literature (e.g. Shakespeare, Chaucer and medieval anonymous works), as well as etymology and the history of English before the eighteenth century. They often also refer to affixes and apply labels. In *EDD Online*, they encourage retrieving etymology via the *etymology* button, or pre-1700 references to time via the *time span* button. They may also help trace historical morphemes, which are excluded in searches applying the *morphemic* filter. However, the text of *comments* is always, except for the *morphemic* filter, included in the result of *headword* queries so that queries in *comments* seem largely redundant.

Yet they are not. They keep information on the sometimes incalculable historical background of LModE dialect words separate. In view of this background, users may often not have a clear concept of what they might be looking for. Given the large number of possible sources, background languages, word forms and abbreviations, the principle of serendipity comes into play. Users may search through the comments under the aspects of any of the filters offered in combination with them. These filters are etymology, usage labels, sources, morphemic and time spans. It seems fair to assume that many an historical insight concerning the pre-1700 life of English dialect words can be triggered that way. To start off, simply type in the strings of your historical interest and search for them in the *comments* mode.

In addition to the comments at the end of entries just described, Wright, as mentioned earlier, has occasionally marked shorter passages within the running text using brackets, thereby downgrading their relevance. Sometimes these passages are normalised versions of broad dialect, sometimes semantic explanations of terms or the like. In our XML marking, we have always adapted these 'minor' comments to their textual surroundings, no matter whether these happened to be definitions or citations. Thus, even information of minor relevance in the *EDD* has not been lost.

7.6   Variants

Most of the *variants* that have been tagged by us as such are – as in the *Oxford English Dictionary* – phonological and spelling variants, but there are also some generally lexical or semantic 'variants', i.e. synonyms or homophones/ polysemes. In either case, Wright has used phrases such as 'also in the form of', 'also written as', 'the same word as', and the like to introduce the variants. In the *Supplement* (published in 1905 as part of vol. 6) he also, for whatever reason, newly used the Latin abbreviation 'i.q.', which stands for 'idem quid' and means 'the same as'. While the borderline between lexemes and their variants is fuzzy in the *EDD*, which is also attested by some lemmatised variants, the good news is that the button *variants* now encourages studying the principles of variation in dialect, as well as identifying unknown strange forms.

To relate *variants* to *dialect areas*, users may activate the dialect filters, like with the other parameters. As regards other filters, *variants* can also be combined with *etymology, usage labels* and *time spans*. Technically, even the combination with *sources* is feasible, but again, as with *citations*, query outputs have to be checked manually because the selected source may not, on closer inspection, really refer to the variant at issue, but only happens to occur in the same entry.[2]

Figure 7.9 demonstrates a search for *variants* beginning with *y-*, combined with the time span from 1800 to 1900. This query delivers those variants for the headwords of which there is nineteenth-century evidence via the dates of the sources in the entry concerned.

The search of Figure 7.9 is motivated by the role of so-called *j*-insertion, which Markus examined in a paper some years ago (2011). This dialectal deviation from the English Standard, a phenomenon complementary to *h*-dropping, was common practise in the nineteenth century so that the

---

[2] Despite this lack of reliability, we decided to tolerate the 'fuzzy logic' of the combination with *sources* because in this way researchers interested in variants have at least a frame of reference to start from.

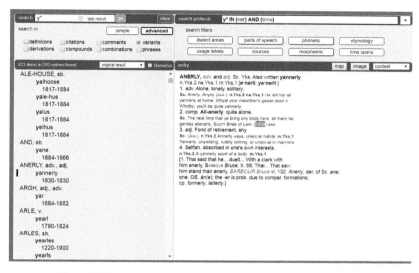

Figure 7.9 Parameter *variants* combined with *time span* 1800–1900

823 examples found in our query do not come as a surprise.[3] The spelling of this palatal fricative /j/, inserted before word-initial vowels, was *y-*.[4]

7.7   Derivations

While Wright's concept of derivations was surprisingly correct, there are some contestable cases where the bound quality of a prefix or suffix may be questioned. We did not have time to reflect such matters of terminology theoretically nor did we consider interpretations of our own, but generally followed Wright, who, in the *EDD*, usually introduces derivations by the introductory marker *hence*. In rare cases, however, *hence* has also been used for the introduction of clearly other types of word formation, for example, *combinations*. In our work, this was no great problem as long as the types were kept separate within an entry. However, occasionally the *EDD* provides different groups of word formation under the heading 'hence', or some equivalent heading. In such cases, we tagged this *hence*, or whatever other introductory marker, by the XML cover tag 'mix_intro' and the serial numbers as 'mix_num'.

Despite this difficulty in our work of grasping different types of word formation correctly, these are now neatly kept apart – see Figure 7.10.

---

[3] About half of these matches, however, are *y*-initial forms that are not due to *j*-insertion.
[4] Also see the more detailed discussion of this fricative in Section 8.3.1.

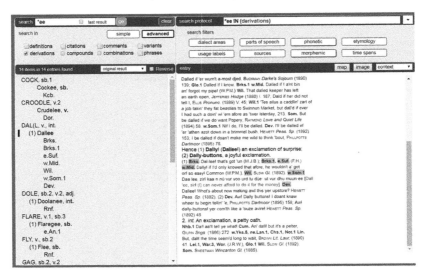

Figure 7.10 Search for *derivations* ending in *-ee*

Figure 7.10, based on *-ee* as an example, shows us a result of fourteen matches. The entry DAL(L includes the derivation *Dallee*, but also the compound *Dally-buttons*, both under the heading 'Hence'. Our software has rightly selected *Dallee* and the dialect areas referring to it under number (1). A search for *dal**, as part of a derivation, would also only provide *Dally (Dallee)*, but not the compound *Dally-buttons*. This would only appear after a query for *compounds*.

As regards compatibility, the parameter *derivations* permits a combination with all filters except *phonetic* and *morphemic*. The exclusion of *phonetic* stands to reason – word formation operates on a different level than the analysis of sounds. *Morphemic* is excluded because this filter provides a limited selection of bound morphemes, thus not being compatible with the free-choice strings of the search box in the case of derivations being at issue.

Readers who are interested in the morphology of derivations would be concerned with this filter *morphemic*, which offers a list of the most common bound lexical pre- and suffixes. The advantage of this filter is that it not only finds derivations **within** entries (and marked as such, like *Dallee* in Figure 7.10) but also headwords that happen to be derivations. The search for *-ee* in the filter mode would have provided a much larger number of matches (namely 456). The disadvantage of this option, however, is that not all **ee*-forms are valid matches (as in *tree*). Further details on the filter *morphemic* are discussed in Section 6.3.7.

7.8 Compounds

The introductory marker in the *EDD* is 'Also in comp.' or, simply, 'In comp.'. The high frequency of this marker is in line with the observation that dialects are extremely creative, even hyper-productive in compounding (see Markus 2012). Accordingly, compounds in the *EDD* may be a very promising field of study in dialectology.

The fact that Wright also uses the technical term 'combination', similar in meaning to 'compound', tackles the question of how 'compounds' can be defined versus 'combinations'. The question will be dealt with in the next section, but one feature of definition should be tackled here. Hyphenation is a non-reliable criterion of a 'compound'. After all, Wright was mainly confronted with spoken dialect use and, thus, obviously found it difficult or impossible to decide in individual cases whether a compound had to be hyphenated when written down, or not. His quotations confirm the generally inconsistent use of hyphens in dialect texts. Accordingly, the hyphens actually used in practically all *EDD* compounds – very short ones so that they could almost be addressed as points – are, as mentioned earlier (Section 2.2), ambiguously bi-functional: they always mark the morphemic border between the constituents of compounds, in most, but not all cases additionally suggesting hyphens.

This ambiguity has naturally affected our interpretation of the hyphens used for line-breaking as well as for abbreviating purposes, i.e. Wright's substitution of a determinant or determinatum in a compound by '-'. For example, rather than listing all lexemes with the determinatum *-house* in full, Wright, after the first sample, has only printed out the determinants and has abbreviated the second element (the determinatum): *dog-, pig-,* etc. For determinants spelt separately, or for separate elements of phrases, he has used a dash (–). As regards the first point, hyphens, there has been no way of mechanically disambiguating their double function at the end of lines.

As mentioned earlier, the general structural overlaps between *compounds* and the other two types of word formation (*combinations* and *phrases*) should be considered in all compound queries. Our interface technically allows for queries combining *compounds*, *combinations* and *derivations*. In particular, users interested in compounds are advised to include the data classified and tagged by us, in line with Wright, as 'combinations'.

As regards computer retrieval, all hyphens and dashes representing compound elements have been replaced by the constituents they stand for.[5]

---

[5] After initial uncommented insertion we changed our policy – also for other insertions – by marking our editing by {{...}} in the original XML-texts. In the entry windows of the interface,

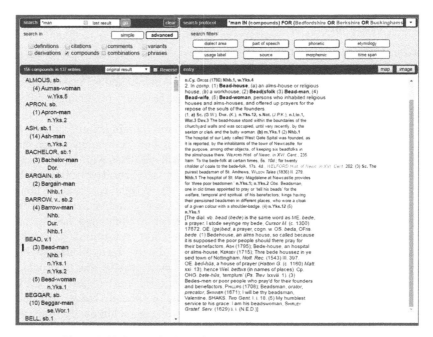

Figure 7.11 Search for *man* in compounds, filtered by 'all English counties'

Given the different positions that compounds may have within entries, we have limited the number of optional combinations with filters to some extent. The filters acceptable with compounds are *dialect areas, usage labels, etymology, sources* and *time spans*. Note that the *dialect areas*, when not specified by the user, are by default added in the retrieval output. They can then also be identified on our maps in the usual way. As with headwords, the *original-result* output can also be re-arranged according to areas, with counties, regions and nations, in this case of non-specified dialect areas, jointly listed alphabetically.[6]

While such queries, unspecified for dialect, are helpful for raising survey issues, users will usually wish to specify both the search string and the dialect area(s). In the example of Figure 7.11, the search string *man,* combined with the filter 'all English counties', has produced 156 matches.

---

these parentheses are automatically deleted and the strings concerned instead appear in a light grey.

[6] I.e. West Country (region) follows Warwickshire (county), which follows Wales (nation).

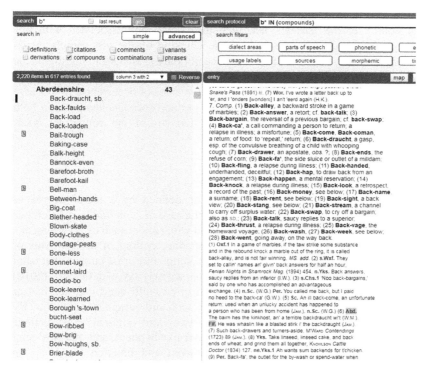

Figure 7.12 Presentation of background knowledge of the interface: compounds with *b** arranged county-wise

Again, the *original-result* box of Figure 7.11 allows for sorting modes other than the one presented. The matches can be arranged in six further types, for example, as compounds from A to Z or by dialect areas. The list also includes options for hierarchising the data. *Column 2 with 3* arranges the data by compounds, adding the dialect areas for each of the compounds and counting them both as tokens and types. *Column 3 with 2*, on the other hand, alphabet-ises the areas (e.g. counties) and individually attributes and counts the compounds. As with headwords, the names of areas are normalised (in spelling), and the frequencies of occurrence can be mapped in four different modes, from 'absolute' to 'relative per 10,000', with the term 'relative' implying the relation to the overall frequency figures of the areas concerned. Even in this specified presentation mode *column 3 with 2*, the presented compounds are clickable in such a way that users do not only find the selected compound itself but also the dialect areas affiliated with it in the background. This may be illustrated in Figure 7.12.

The sorting mode shown in Figure 7.12 has triggered Aberdeenshire as the first county of the retrieval list, with the compounds associated with this county in alphabetical order underneath. Clicking on the first sample, *back-draucht*, the entry window of the interface not only presents and highlights the context of the compound in the text, but also – see the reddish (here: grey) marks in the bottom half of the citations – the areas of occurrence, in this case *Abd.* and *Fif.* (for 'Fife'). As one can see, our software has again traced both these counties in line with the *numerus currens* of the compound *back-draucht*, number (6).

7.9   Combinations

Combinations can, in a first approach, be defined by a lower degree of connection between their elements than in the case of *compounds*, a difference which tendentially seems to go hand in hand with factors such as (a) young age of the expression concerned, (b) (still) separate spelling of the elements of combinations and (c) the lack of the typical compound stress pattern, that is, of the initial stress.[7] In addition to these features we may say with Onysko (2010) that 'combinations' in Wright's sense tend to be multi-word non-nominal or only partly nominal constructions, usually with orthographic separation. By contrast, 'compounds' are nearly always 'two-word nominal' constructions with 'orthographic unity' (if we ignore the dot-like hyphen), and 'phrases' tend to be constructions of three or more 'content and function words … in orthographic separation' (2010: 143).

Which of the filters do *combinations* allow? The answer is, the same as the *compounds*: *dialect areas, usage labels, etymology, sources* and *time spans*.

The important role of *combinations* side by side with *compounds* in the *EDD* can be assumed in the face of the surprisingly high number of output matches in the query shown in Figure 7.13: 131 occurrences for just one word. The search string (*man*) and the filter (all *English counties*) are the same as we used them for *compounds*, where the result figure was only insignificantly higher (156).

As with the query for *compounds* in Figure 7.11, our search string **man* in Figure 7.13 has only word-initial truncation. As a result, we have only been searching for *man* as the final morpheme of combinations (the *determinatum*). Findings such as *man-slaughter* were excluded in this way. Accordingly, our lists of compounds and combinations in Figures 7.11 and 7.13 are not

---

[7] Given that we are here discussing features of spoken language, I have no evidence for this statement in the *EDD*, but only by extrapolating from Present-Day English. Newly coined terms such as *business manager* and *computer program* are still stressed by some with an at least secondary word accent on the second element, i.e. the *determinatum*.

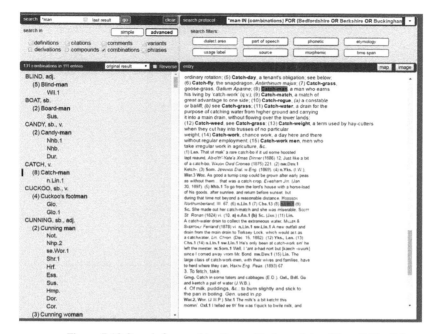

Figure 7.13 Search for *combinations* with **man* (plus filter *all English counties*)

complete. The seemingly all-inclusive search for "man" (without truncation) delivers 137 combinations and 184 compounds. This query, then, grabs more matches, but it is not really all-inclusive either. While it rightly excludes *woman* and *manner*, it also wrongly excludes valid forms such as *man's*. Like good craftsmen, users have to be able to find out which tool to use for which purpose.

Before we leave the parameter of *combinations*, it seems worth repeating that this parameter for its part can be combined with *compounds* and *derivations* in one query. We have implemented this facility mainly because, as mentioned, Wright's division between the three categories is not always linguistically reliable.

7.10   Phrases

Given Onysko's definition, mentioned in the last section, that 'phrases' in the *EDD* are three or more 'content and function words ... in orthographic separation' (2010: 143), the modern, more strictly syntactic definition of

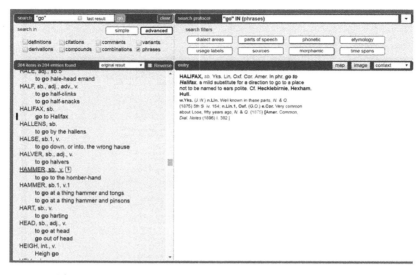

Figure 7.14 Search for phrases with (non-truncated) *go*

'phrase' should be left aside.[8] Clearly Wright's prototypical concept of a 'phrase' aims at multi-word idiomatic expressions, similes and proverbs (cf. Onysko 2010: 143). Accordingly, users interested in phrasal verbs, for example, should try to find them under both *phrases* and *combinations*.

Notwithstanding this warning, Figure 7.14 presents an example which may demonstrate the prolific role of common verbs in the formation of phrases.

The 384 matches partly shown in Figure 7.14 may give rise to the assumption that phrases, in the particular shape of 'composite predicates',[9] play a more important role in dialects than in the English Standard. Moreover, the motivation of these phrases often seems to be rather local – cf. the example opened in the entry window (*to go to Halifax*). In the Standard, on the other hand, phrasal verbs, based on more universal metaphorisation of postpositions (*to go for, to go by* etc.), are the more typical subclass. Admittedly, this is a mere hypothesis, which will have to be tested in future in-depth investigations. However, in a paper focusing on special similes as a subset of phrases, I concluded that 'most of them are relatively transparent, stemming from the rural sphere or based on traditional habits' (Markus 2010a: 214). This result would support the suspicion that dialectal phrases are, by and large, more

---

[8] I am here thinking of specifically focused studies of the type of Brinton and Akimoto (1999).

[9] For the theory of this structure (type: *to go for a walk*) and for its role in the history of English, see Brinton and Akimoto (1999), and my review of this book in *Anglia* 122 (2004): 491–4.

locally and less universally motivated than those of the Standard variety of English.

The parameter *phrases* allows for the same optional filters as the *compounds* and *combinations*, i.e. *dialect areas, etymology, usage labels, sources* and *time spans,* all of these with a large number of sub-filters in them. The filter *usage labels,* for example, encourages the selection of figurative/metaphorical phrases, to give just one example. Irrespective of the specific sub-filters, searching for *phrases* means that users type in a string as part of the expected phrases and get them in their complete extension.

Wright has sometimes syntactically merged two or more manifestations of an idiomatic pattern into a sequence of strings, for example, in '*to go down,* or *into, the wrong hause*' (in Figure 7.14, under HALSE), meaning 'to go down the wrong way in the throat'. In such elliptical cases we have usually separated the two phrases at issue, but in extreme cases like the one just quoted we may have shied away from the labour-intensive task of expanding the phrasal relics, instead marking the merged whole as only one phrase (with variation).

As with the other *advanced* parameters, the parameter of *phrases* allows for result lists to be arranged according to seven different sorting options. These options can be activated after a result list of a query has been generated, but also beforehand. In the latter case, the time needed for searches is greatly extended.

7.11   Survey: Compatibility of Parameters with Filters

Table 7.1 provides a survey of the various possible combinations of parameters and filters. Only the *headwords* can be combined with all available filters. In *full text,* this combination would not make sense since it would not be clear what a string triggered by a filtered query refers to within an entry. In other words, *full text* generally interprets the text as an unstructured conglomerate of strings.[10]

The four lexemic types *compounds, combinations, derivations* and *phrases* can all be combined with *dialect areas, usage labels, sources, etymology* and *time spans,* but the button *derivations,* in addition, allows for a combination with *parts of speech.* For example, users may wish to search for adjectives versus adverbs ending in –*ly,* thus checking the productivity of this suffix for the two word classes.

Indirectly the combination of *derivations* with the filter *morphemic* is also acceptable because this filter automatically activates *derivations* in addition to *headwords,* given that no parameter has previously been clicked. As in all

---

[10] Cf., however, the exception of *full text* searches for phonetic signs eligible in the filter *phonetic* (Section 6.3.6).

Table 7.1 *Survey of possible combinations of parameters and filters*

param.\filter	dial.	pos	phon	etym	labels	sources	morph	time
headword	x	x	x	x	x	x	x	x
full text			(x)					
compounds	x			x	x	x		x
derivations	x	x		x	x	x	(x)	x
combinations	x			x	x	x		x
phrases	x			x	x	x		x
definitions	x			x	x	x		
citations	x			x	x	x		x
comments				x	x	x	(x)	x
variants	x			x	x			x

query cases, the search protocol documents the content of the query, in this case its automatically activated target: *headword* and *derivations*. Note that this search routine only allows for those search strings of affixes which are listed in the filter *morphemic*.

While *definitions* can only be combined with *dialect areas, sources, etymology* and *labels* – the latter with its special semantic option allowing access to flora and fauna –, *citations* additionally allows for combinations with the filters of *time span*.

Comments and *variants* share their compatibility with the filters *etymology*, *usage label* and *time span*. *Comments*, moreover, permits a combination with *sources* and – in a limited way – *morphemic*,[11] whereas *variants* is, naturally, of interest in relation to *dialect areas*.

In this verbalised description, the permitted correlations may perhaps seem confusing and somewhat arbitrary. But they are not. For obvious reasons, the two main filters in a historical dialect dictionary are place and time of a dialect word or string, i.e. the *dialect area* and the years of its use (*time span*). The almost ubiquitous role of *etymology* as a filter does justice to the fact that Wright, at the end of entries, often refers to cognates of the headword concerned. *Compounds* and the other types of lexemic composition participate in such etymological backgrounds of the headwords, though the etymological forms given do not, strictly speaking, specifically refer to them. This slight fuzziness of correlation also seemed acceptable in the case of the *time span*

---

[11] As the filter *morphemic* refers to headwords and derivations, it is not really compatible with the parameter *comments*. Nevertheless, we have not cancelled the filter's accessibility (in red) to allow the user to see the two lists of prefixes and suffixes and to borrow any of these affixes as a search string. The *comments* are often concerned with affixes.

filter. As mentioned, only the sources are directly characterised by time. All other parameters that can likewise be combined with *time span* in any case do so indirectly via the date of publication or edition of a source text.

The fourth dominant filter is that of the *usage labels*. This filter plays quite an important role in relation to practically all structural units of the *Dictionary*, from the *headwords* to the *variants*. Only *full text* is too amorphous a category to encourage filter combination – *phonetic* is the only filter implemented with it because the few phonetic transcriptions that do not refer to *headwords* are unpredictably spread all over the entries.

Finally, it should be said once more that some of the filters may be of interest in themselves, i.e. without the combination with any parameter or string. In the filter of *sources*, it would, thus, be feasible to search for a particular work or author, for example, Shakespeare or Dickens and get all the works/passages connected with that name no matter what parameter this literary name mentioned refers to. After a query of this kind, the headword concerned (plus its part of speech) will always be provided, but nothing else – unless the user has combined the filter *sources* with a second filter, say, with *dialect areas*. It would then perhaps be of interest to see where Dickens, or whichever other name or text, has been quoted most. By the same token, labels can be searched for irrespective of any parameter. Such filter-only queries seem sensible in all those cases where the sub-menus of the filters arouse the user's curiosity. Only the *time span* filter had better not be used in isolation because a year as such is hardly interpretable without its cotext within an entry.

8 Research Issues Encouraged by *EDD Online*

Recently, there have been some promising studies on regional dialects in English-speaking countries, for example, Braber and Robinson (2018) on East Midland English, published within the *Dialects of English* series by Walter de Gruyter. However, nearly all of these publications, including those of the series mentioned, refer to English varieties outside England. By and large, the study of traditional English dialects cannot claim in 2019 to be a mainstream field of English linguistics, at least not to the extent that it did in former university teaching. Certainly, one of the reasons is the predominant interest in sociolinguistics, particularly in England and the US.[1] This strong interest can be interpreted as an answer to the growing role of social factors, classes and awareness in our Western world since the nineteenth century. Another reason for the loss of prestige of traditional dialects is the new focus on the 'many Englishes' worldwide, which is mainly due to the Western post-colonial heritage and now, more generally, to globalisation. These trends, detrimental to a scholarly interest in traditional dialectology, have been enhanced by the great weight of synchronic linguistics in contrast to diachronic linguistics in this and the last centuries. Traditional dialects have always been rooted in diachronic linguistics and also for this reason have lost curricular ground.[2]

In the face of this rather desolate situation, the question is how the role of English dialectology can be strengthened and improved. This raises the more general issue of why dialectology should matter. This chapter, initially, discusses such general questions. Then, in the subsequent Sections 3–7, we use seven parameters/filters offered by *EDD Online* as test cases of the scholarly work that is now feasible.

---

[1] Scotland, Ireland and Wales, however, are different, with many projects and publications as evidence; cf., for example, *The Linguistic Atlas of Scotland* 2010; *Linguistic Atlas and Survey of Irish Dialects* 1958, repr. 1981; Parry, *Survey of Anglo-Welsh Dialects*, 2 vols., 1977 and 1979.

[2] Research on language change has, since the late 1900s, focused on the theory of change, generally viewing the neogrammarian methods sceptically and soon turning to the impact of social factors on language change. A good example is McMahon (1994: 226–32).

8.1   Why Study Dialectology?

Why study dialectology? W. Nelson Francis, in his valuable and still valid introduction (1983: 7), offers four kinds of motivation, which he calls 'the curious, the anthropological, the linguistic, and the practical'. The quotation suggests the far-reaching complexity of dialectology, even in the (older) narrow sense of regional dialects that Francis still has in mind. But to understand the first three catch-word categories ('the curious, the anthropological, the linguistic'), Francis's subsequent statements seem worth referring to: dialect implies ethnic humour ('essentially innocent humour' [Francis 1983: 7]), and 'language differences are often indicators of deep-seated social and cultural phenomena' (Francis 1983: 8), which are bound to have various repercussions in everyday life, for example, school life. All these aspects concern the non-linguistic aspects of dialectology, from 'the curious' to 'the practical'.

The remaining linguistic motivation, as Francis goes on to explain, deals with 'points of pronunciation, grammar, meaning, and vocabulary not as isolated phenomena, but as parts of an elaborately integrated system' (1983: 9). The value of this approach, to be contrasted to the questionable understanding that dialect is 'something rather messy and embarrassing' (9), cannot be overestimated. In addition, dialects 'are often a source of valuable evidence to the historical linguist' (9).

Many linguists would probably sign this understanding of dialectology as a complex linguistic discipline with many interdisciplinary implications concerning pragmatics as well as the social, anthropological and practical embedding of dialect speech. But my impression is that dialectology in practice is still a rather specialised and narrow-focused sub-discipline of linguistics, downgraded by less traditional and more modern or modish fields. What we have is details of word geography and of phonetic variation, sometimes also of syntactic variation, but the 'rules' behind the phenomena, the conditioning factors – language-internal or language-external – have only rarely been topicalised.[3]

I hope that the data provided by *EDD Online* are apt to improve the situation. The information is so flexibly available and, due to Wright's concept of language as a social and cultural phenomenon, so much embedded in human and historical contextuality that users will feel encouraged to raise many new questions that they have not been able to ask up to now. Before I give a few examples of this ambitious inter- and intradisciplinary approach, a short

---

[3] Some titles may stand here for the general state of the art: Orton and Wright 1974; Kolb et al. 1979; Kortmann et al. 2005; Upton and Widdowson 2006; Viereck and Ramisch 1991–1997.

glimpse may be cast at the main weakness of the type of dialectology in the last decades: the unjustified predominance of word geography.

8.2   Dialect Is More Than Words

Popular dialect dictionaries, and present-day dialectology in general, may misleadingly suggest that dialect is mainly a matter of dialect words used instead of the standard ones.[4] But *EDD Online* makes it clear that dialect is much more than the distribution of words and their pronunciation across space and that dialectology is concerned with practically all levels of the language system and, moreover, many aspects of usage. The role of special words is just the most obvious (and superficial) feature of dialect speech. The members of the Innsbruck project team have equipped the diverse pieces of information in our XML-version of the *EDD* entries with a large number of tags, in line with the general wealth and variance of dialect features in the language system.

The first group of tags is concerned with the formal features of a dialect lemma: its function in terms of word class; its syntactic function, for example, as a participle or transitive word; its formal variation in spelling and pronunciation; its usage description, for example, concerning its frequency or degree of obsolescence; and, finally, its spatial and temporal features.

The second group of tags focuses on the meanings of lemmas or phraseologisms. In an earlier paper (Markus 2012), I argued that dialect speech is particularly prone to coin word compositions, that is, compounds, derivations and phrases. Wright even needed a new term for newly coined compositions (between compounds and phrases, as it were). These were compositions that were not yet as established as compounds but were idiomatically more fixed than phrases. Wright used the term 'combination' for this type of word formation. Word combinations of a 'risky' type, such as *the-man-I-met-yesterday's hat*, are, of course, not uncommon in Present-Day English (cf. Leisi and Mair on the role of the 'Wortverband' ['word cluster'] in Present-Day English [1999: 74ff.]). However, the example just given is certainly stylistically marked as colloquial everyday speech – which brings us back, or at least close to, the speech of dialect. I tried to show that dialect speech is particularly

---

[4] Cf., on the one hand, survey publications such as the *English Dialect Atlas* by Viereck et al. (2002). On the other hand, several books have been published on dialect geography, particularly in the American and German research scene – cf. Carver (1989), *American Regional Dialects: A Word Geography*; Ernst (2008), *Dialektgeographie der Zukunft*; Kaiser (1937), *Zur Geographie des mittelenglischen Wortschatzes*. Also cf. the structure of the *Deutsches Wörterbuch* by Jacob and Wilhelm Grimm, as digitised by the *Excellence Centre* of the University of Trier. The (often extremely long) entries can only be retrieved as a whole, but not according to specific parameters. Cross-references can, it is true, be targeted by links. However, by and large, the information accessible always refers to individual entries.

productive in spontaneous and often rather emotional coinings of new compositions, as it seems most inventive in the creation of metaphors (Markus 2012). This strategy of using the words already available in the language for coining new ones goes hand in hand with the tendential avoidance of Latinate or generally 'hard' words.

The *EDD*'s wealth in matters of word formation and 'derived' meanings affiliated with a lemma is, therefore, not surprising. The *EDD* contains some 71,484 lemmas in 64,486 entries (excluding the Supplement), but, in addition, 15,830 compounds, 21,583 combinations, 6,469 phrases and, moreover, 11,636 derivations. If all these had been listed separately and counted as words, the *EDD* would, thus, comprise 127,002 lexemes.

While this adds up to the comprehensive quality of the *EDD*, its complexity is mainly caused by homophony and polyphony: identical word forms have different meanings, depending on cotext and context. The *EDD* reveals an enormous ambition in the subtlety of its semantic and pragmatic analysis. Some entries list more than a hundred meanings. To limit the complexity, Wright has also subsumed grammatical 'meanings' here, such as the multiple functions of a verb's participle or a noun's plural form. As mentioned, the complexity is raised by the inclusion of pragmatic aspects. These have been categorised by us as labels to keep the level of usage somewhat apart from the level of the language system. Of course, Wright did not mark such aspects as 'pragmatic', but most regularly used introductory formulas such as 'applied by (children, women)' or 'applied to (old people, dogs, etc.)'. We have highly appreciated such formulas as initial markers of pragmatic relevance. It remains to be seen to what extent these markers could be evaluated on the sociolinguistic level.

Our interface displays further segments of the entries for retrieval routines, beyond the types of word formation. One of them, equally important, is that of the *variants*. For England alone the *Dictionary* lists 36,930 variants, for Scotland 16,713 and so on. Users of *EDD Online* can, of course, search for specific variants, but they can also truncate strings to find, for example, variants beginning with a *y*- or ending in -*in*, thus producing lists of words with such variants, accompanied by the headwords belonging to them. An even more interesting routine would be the combination of variant searches with some of the filters. The filters allow for generating lists of all the variants of a certain region or period or label, or whatever other filter may seem appropriate, both in isolation and in combination with each other.

It is also possible to combine the class of *variants* with that of the *headwords* and thus, by way of areal filters, generate areal glossaries. This is achieved by using the *last-result* button. This button, on top of the retrieval window, re-activates the *headword* results of a previous query to be the *quorum* on which to start a new query. For example, the combination of *headwords* with *usage labels*, say 'curse', produces 224 results of headwords, which means that the entries of these headwords somewhere contain an abbreviation/term for swearing. Then it may occur to the user to start a new query on this subset of entries to find out which of these headwords are affiliated with *God* as a term of definition, that is, the user is interested in finding out about the abuse of the name of God in swearing. All one has to do is to type *God* in the search box, setting the hook for the *last result* and activating *definitions* in the *advanced* mode, and then click on *go*. In next to no time 32 hits are presented, a subset of the 224 earlier entries. One may also, after a first search, switch to the *last-result* mode and start a new query for the dialects concerned, by activating, say, all English dialects (178 matches). It is, thus, possible to apply complex combinations of criteria that would not have been feasible in the first place. One could, for example, further filter the list of matches for time. The gist of these (repeated) last-result queries is that users are always limiting their searches to the subset of headwords/entries previously found, even if the new search focuses on something else than these headwords.

While it is true that the *last-result* mode does not allow for any imaginable combinations that do not make sense, it allows users to 'outwit' the system. To remain with our example of curses referring to God, the parameter of *definitions* is itself not compatible with the filter of *time spans*. However, once the curses with the implicit references to God have been found (plus their headwords), the list of headwords concerned can be used for a new (*last-result*) query by the user switching on the filter of *time span*. All that is needed is to switch this filter on again after its having been blocked for searches of *definitions* and then to click on the *last-result* button twice, once for de-activating it, and the second time, after changing the search string from 'God' to an asterisk and the search parameter from *definitions* back to *headwords*, for its re-activation. The query will now target the thirty-two headwords of the retrieval list and generate a subset list of twenty-three headwords, with the time spans added (I selected the nineteenth century).

The *last-result* mode allows for optionally repeated specification. The rule of thumb for using it, therefore, is (1) search only for a parameter that is equal to, or more specific than, the previous one (e.g. first *headwords*, then *definitions* [within the entries of these headwords]). Once you have specified your query, you cannot de-specify it on the same level because you cannot regain the lost entries. The re-iterated specification has to take place on different levels. The result of the twenty-three headwords above, for example, could further be filtered for parts of speech, say, for interjections. Note that result lists and the protocols of a subsequent query only present the concerns of that query, but not the findings of the previous ones, which function as data analysed in the background.

The *last-result* mode may seem slightly confusing when first applied, yet it allows the complexity of queries to be carried to quite an extreme and proves that the potential of *EDD Online* goes far beyond the mere retrieval of words. It is this openness of our interface in the face of new challenging aspects of English dialects that make it a most valuable tool.

The rest of this chapter is given to concrete examples of what seem to me to be sensible analyses. We will test some of the parameters, that is, options on the left side of the interface, in relation to some of the filters, that is, options on the right side.

8.3   Test Cases for Scholarly Work with *EDD Online*

8.3.1   *Towards Searching for Variants*

One of the search units provided by our interface as a parameter is *variants*. The variants explicitly provided by Wright are mostly to be understood as spelling variants, but the *EDD* has also quite a few variants in the citations that are interpretable mainly as 'pseudo-phonetic' spellings. Such spellings, i.e. spellings somehow suggestive of the pronunciation, had quite a tradition in the nineteenth century until the impact of the norm triggered by the API (*Association Phonétique Internationale*) in the late 1880s. Wright's own phonetic transcription in the *EDD* was an approximate anticipation of this norm, but his predecessors, whose sources are quoted galore, had often subjective modes of pseudo-phonetic spellings of their own. Notwithstanding the differences between these various spelling-modes, we of the *EDD Online* project have grasped all these spellings expressing variants under the heading *variants*.

For the sake of illustration, I suggest selecting *h*-dropping as a topic illustrating the role of variants. Dropping one's aitches has become one of the dominant features of speech marked for dialect and sociolect. Accordingly, this feature has met with great scholarly interest. I have tackled it myself when *EDD Online* was not yet available (Markus 2002). My paper focused on the history of *h*-dropping rather than on its Late Modern English distribution. In a later paper, I emphasised the connection of *h*-dropping with *h*-insertion and, moreover, *j*-insertion (*yale* instead of *ale*; Markus 2011). Now that EDD Online is finished in its third version (2019), it is time for revisiting the whole issue.

H-dropping is the loss of *h* (aitch) in stressed syllables at the beginning of words. But how can we find the words concerned? Searching for words beginning with vowels is to no avail because the list of matches contains many unstressed syllables and words which never before had a word-initial *h*, such as the conjunction *and*. Here we could expect *h*-insertion (*hand*). There is still the question of how *h*-droppings can be retrieved in *EDD Online*.

Before we start, one query option mentioned on various earlier occasions needs to be explained in some detail. It opens on top of the retrieval window after a query has been run and is called *original result* in the default mode. This default mode provides the matches in the order of the *Dictionary's* headwords concerned. The first alternative option is *column 1 a-z*. Since all queries present their results with the headwords concerned at the top of the hierarchical structure of the retrieval lists, *column 1* always refers to the headwords. The alphabetisation within this mode allows the user to focus on headwords beginning with a specific letter, for example, with an <h>, and check the results listed as variants in *column 2* and subordinated to these headwords. We can, thus, see that the headword *HAAR* has *aar* as a variant, *HAB* has *ab*, and so on. However, this presentation mode of *column 1 a-z* urges users to glean the examples of *h*-dropping (or *h*-insertion, for that matter) from the retrieval list. This is the manual method I had to apply myself in Markus (2011). However, in addition to these basic modes of presentation, which were already available in earlier versions of *EDD Online*, the present version 3.0 allows users, in the case of multi-column results of a query, to isolate, alphabetise and quantify the retrieval lists of the second to fourth columns. The tool of quantification was only recently (2018) implemented in our interface.[5]

But to start the demonstration, we now begin with a simple search for *headwords* with initial <ha> – the number of the output is 1,202. To find the variants with dropped aitches, we, in a first step, apply a *last-result* search for *variants* with word-initial <a>. The interface finds 184 items (i.e. variants with *a**) in 103 entries, with the headwords, a subset of the 1,202 headwords of the first query, listed alphabetically. Figure 8.1 illustrates this step.

Of course, we have to go through the same procedure for the other vowels <e, i, o, u> and <y> – the interface does not 'know' what a 'vowel' is, and they may all be of relevance. Moreover, for some headwords with initial <h>, Wright has illustrated the *h*-less forms not by mentioning such variants, but by giving the phonetic transcription. Thus, the headword HABIT is phonetically transcribed as [a·bit.]. The interface provides thirty-eight samples of this type, with none of them doubly marked by both a phonetic transcription and a variant form. We can, therefore, add the thirty-eight findings to the 184 items of the first query for *h*-less variants. However. we will ignore these extra tasks

---

[5] There is a further alternative option that allows for the analysis of the findings in the reverse mode, i.e. with the word 'way', for example, alphabetically interpreted from tail to head, as if it was 'yaw', so that words with the same final morpheme or suffix (and phrases with the same final word) are listed together in the output of a query. As in other reverse dictionaries this mode allows interesting research on phonotactic features such as rhyme, and on morphological issues, for example, concerning derivations.

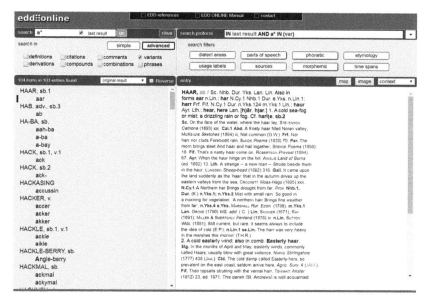

Figure 8.1 Search for English variants of ha* with word-initial <a> (*last-result* mode)

here, focusing our present interest on the pseudo-phonetic spellings alone and the next main steps.

The next step is correlating the 184 variants of Figure 8.1 to dialect areas. Figure 8.2 shows us the result of a query based on all dialect areas available in the interface, that is, all *counties*, *regions* and *nations*.

With regard to the retrieval list, the user will soon find that the arrangement according to headwords (*original result* or *column 1 a-z*) is of little help in providing a real survey on dialectal distribution of *h*-droppings. To obtain such a survey, users may rearrange the three-column results according to their needs. 'Column' is our neutral term for the three hierarchical slots (headwords, variants and dialect areas) involved, and partly visible, in Figure 8.2. The options of re-arrangement, now available, can be seen in Figure 8.3, which shows the run-down menu with overall seven different types of assortment.

As the last three options show, column 3, that is, the column of dialect references, may rank highest in three different ways. *Column 3 counted* helps provide statistics, with a focus on the areal distribution. Using *column 3 with 1* implies that the dialect areas again come first, with the headwords concerned subordinated, so that one can see at a glimpse which words are concerned by *h*-dropping in Lincolnshire or any other area. Finally, *column 3 with 2*

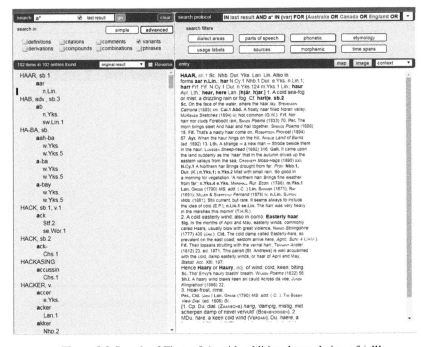

Figure 8.2 Search of Figure 8.1, with additional correlation of 'all' dialect areas

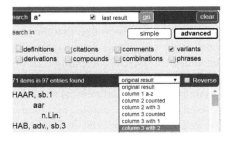

Figure 8.3 Run-down menu for different assortment routines available

correlates areas with the variants themselves rather than the headwords. This list would be good enough for checking all the matches of our query and for excluding mismatches. Figure 8.4 demonstrates the last-mentioned of these options, in my view the most interesting one.

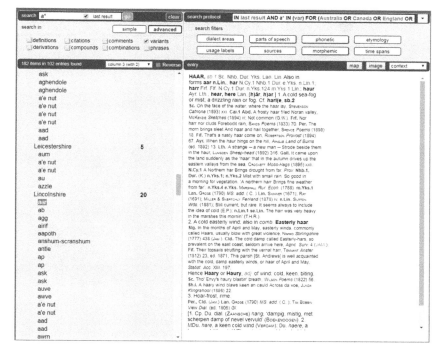

Figure 8.4 Arrangement of the retrieval list of Figure 8.2 (*h*-dropping) area-wise

The quantification of areal references and the corresponding maps are available in all three ways of assortment. Apart from the cartographic means on offer, one of the background achievements of our software is to include every type of dialectal reference, no matter whether by area as such (e.g. *Chs.*) or in the form of a source related to that area (*Ch.1, Chs.12*, etc.). It is also worth mentioning that our software allows for grasping typologically mixed references to areas (counties, regions, nations) in one blow, with the maps simply following track.

The creation of maps based on quantification of dialect references is a fairly complicated matter and will be considered separately below (Chapter 9), in particular, with regard to the expression of degrees of quantity by different (intensities of) colours. However, concerning the distribution of *h*-dropping in the British Isles during the LModE period, the map of Figure 8.5 is meaningful enough to be presented now, allowing for some conclusive observations.

Figure 8.5, in addition to its map on the right, includes a zooming window of the area the user is interested in. I clicked on the county in red, which is the

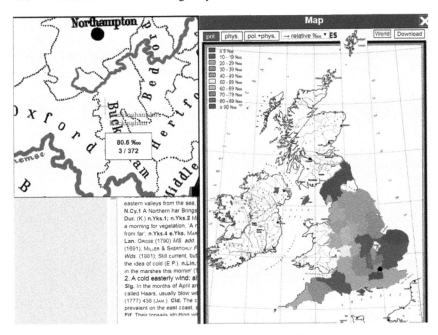

Figure 8.5 *H*-dropping (for <ha->): distribution illustrated on a map of the British Isles (relative per 10,000)

colour standing for a relatively high share of forms with *h*-dropping. The zoomed map not only identifies the county concerned (Buckinghamshire) but also the figures that the pigeonholing of the counties and, thus, the colours are based on.[6]

The results of our test case concerning *h*-dropping are non-spectacular and can be summed up as follows. Based on a per-10,000 mapping, as demonstrated in Figure 8.5, hardly a pattern of regional distribution can be made out. Only Buckinghamshire, Hertfordshire, Shropshire and Herefordshire are remarkably deviant, with their colours standing for more than 50 occurrences per (hypothetical) 10,000. All the other counties have less than fifty points. Strikingly enough, rural areas such as Cumberland, Northumberland and Norfolk are at the low end on the scale of occurrences. On the other hand, Surrey, adjacent to London, is also one of the lilacs (i.e. low-frequency) counties.

---

[6] The pop-up window documents 80.6 per 10,000. This is calculated on the basis of three occurrences of dropped aitch (*a* instead of *ha*), with only 372 references to Buckinghamshire in total.

Apparently searching for the reasons for this distribution does not work on the geographical level alone. We have to include social aspects and the linguistic impact of big industrial cities in our calculus. In Markus (2001), I interpreted my findings concerning Middle English (based on LALME) 'as evidence that previous to, and in addition to, the impulse deriving from French words for *h*-dropping, there was an immanent tendency at work to eliminate initial *h* for phonotactic reasons'. I also argued that, with social factors also playing a role, the general picture of geographical distribution was diffuse 'due to the overlapping of different causal factors'. This result may be taken as a warning that the reasons for *h*-dropping also later were anything but mono-causal. Now returning to Late Modern English, I would suggest two aspects playing an important role within the later history of *h*-dropping: industrialisa-tion, with its growth of the working classes, and the stigmatisation of *h*-drop-ping, started in the eighteenth century and well-known from the late nineteenth and early twentieth (*My Fair Lady*) (Markus 2001). While industrialisation presupposes big cities, the stigmatisation implies the role of neighbouring middle and upper classes prone to look down upon *h*-droppers.

For obtaining a complete picture of *h*-dropping, the diffuse results of Figure 8.5 have to be related to the dialect features somehow connected with *h*-dropping: *h*-insertion, *y*- (or yod-) insertion, and diphthongisation. To keep things simple, we here focus on yod-insertion, that is, the insertion of a /j/, usually spelt <y>, before a stressed word-initial vowel.[7] Figure 8.6 attests to the evidence to be drawn from (the new version 3.0 of) *EDD Online* in the form of a *last result* query.

In Figure 8.6, I have, apart from *yalhoose* for Standard ALE-HOUSE, additionally marked the variant form *yelhus*, to hint at the fact that the spelling *ya*- for Standard *a*- does not cover all possible variants of word-initial stressed *a*-. Apart from *yelhus*, there are further cases of *ye*- (eleven items), and a few cases of *yi*- (two items). Moreover, seven headwords beginning with *ha*** likewise have variant forms with *ya*** (e.g. *hair* as *yar*, *hale* as *yal*), and nine items based on *ha*-initial headwords have *ye*** (e.g. HALFPENNY-WORTH in the variant *yeppath*). Following all these tracks now would certainly go beyond the purpose of this sub-chapter.

However, even the nineteen items of Figure 8.6, only partly visible there, allow for a tentative interpretation. Most of the county-correlated matches for *j*-insertion are inversely proportional to those for *h*-dropping. For example, Buckinghamshire, Hertfordshire, Shropshire and Herefordshire, the counties with a relatively high share of *h*-dropping (according to Figure 8.5), turn out to have zero values with regard to *j*-insertion. On the other hand, some of the nil-, low- or mid-segment counties obtained for *h*-dropping, such as County

---

[7] This issue was dealt with on a statistically less reliable basis (Markus 2011).

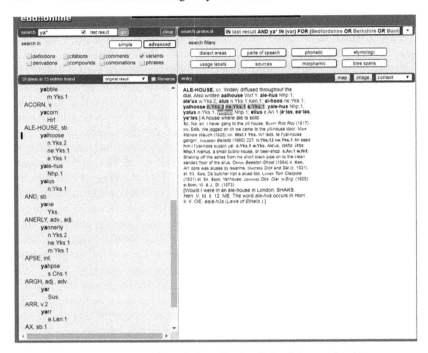

Figure 8.6 Distribution of *j*-insertion in all English counties (focus on *ya*-instead of *a*-)

Durham and Cumberland, have occasional *j*-insertion *ya** for *a** or *ya** for *ha** (Cumberland) or *ye** for *a** (Cumberland, Cheshire, Kent, Surrey) or *ye** for *ha** (Devonshire, Hertfordshire, Northamptonshire). Given these and various other patterns of deviation from the Standard variety, it is not easy to carry out a survey, the more so since the absolute result figures for each of the individual queries are very low. Figure 8.7, however, may demonstrate that there is an immanent trend in the results. The figure contains the results of the last-named option above, *ye** for *ha**.

The map of Figure 8.7 clearly shows that the twenty-one variants with *ye** based on headwords with *ha**, while they are rather rare, are limited to England's South. The map for *ye** from *a**, which may be skipped over here to save space, presents a different, complementary picture, with an additional belt of relevance stretching in the West from Cheshire north to Cumberland and over to Northumberland.

However, the observations of Figures 8.5–8.7 certainly prove that statistics alone, even if refined by normalisation and visualised by maps, can be very confusing as long as we do not ask for the motivation behind the diversity.

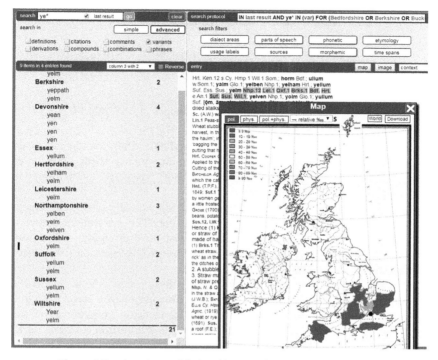

Figure 8.7 *ye*-variants of *ha*, with map of relative distribution (per 10,000)

In the face of the ubiquity of the sound deletions and sound insertions discussed here, it seems fair to assume a general phonotactic motivation. Phonotactically, *h*-dropping is the loss of a 'weak' consonant before a strong (i.e. stressed) vowel, whereas *j*-insertion is the addition of a weak consonant (in this case, half-vowel) before a strong vowel.[8] Both processes are based on the theory that the ideal structure of syllables in English, as in many other languages (e.g. Italian, Japanese) is CV (the sequence consonant–vowel). The diverse phenomena mentioned earlier are connected in that they are all outputs of a combination of a weak consonant with a subsequent strong vowel. *H*, as a particularly weak consonant, may be lost in everyday speech (as the history of various European languages, such as French, proves). On the other hand, etymologically 'naked' vowels (those that were never preceded by an *h*) may be introduced by some previous vowel (thus becoming diphthongs) or by some

[8] With this concept of the 'strength' of consonants and vowels I am arguing in the wake of the phonotactic theories initiated by Vennemann (1988) and Lutz (1991).

entry

ALE-HOUSE, *sb.* Widely diffused throughout the dial. Also written **aalhouse** Wxf.1; **ale-hus** Nhp.1; **ale'us** w.Yks.2; **alus** n.Yks.1 Ken.1; **al-hoos** ne.Yks.1; **yalhoose** n.Yks.2 ne.Yks.1 e.Yks.1; **yale-hus** Nhp.1; **yalus** n.Yks.1; **yelhus** Nhp.1; **ellus** e.An.1 [ē·ləs, eə·ləs, ye·ləs.] A house where ale is sold.
Sc. Na, sir, I never gang to the yill house, SCOTT *Rob Roy* (1817)

Figure 8.8 Variants and phonetic transcriptions of ALE-HOUSE

weak consonant, such as /j/) to introduce the syllable. Such sound changes do not have an identifiable direction, but may be interpreted as the outcome of general disorientation of certain (e.g. dialect) speakers, particularly in fast speech.

In sum, it is socially conditioned, but then phonotactically caused casualness of articulation that we are concerned with here. The general tendency of simplifying articulation may have different results: *h*-dropping, *h*-insertion, *j*-insertion, diphthongisation and, to complete the list, *w*-insertion (here disregarded, but cf. Markus 2011).

H-insertion is, of course, the hypercorrection by speakers who have become aware that *h*-less forms are 'wrong'. *J*-insertion may partly have the same motivation (of hypercorrection), but is also phonotactically conditioned by low and mid-high vowels (i.e. the vowels *a*, *e* and *o*).[9] *W*-insertion concerns back-tongue vowels (cf. URF and URGEE), and diphthongisation, for example, of /e/ to /ie/, is the fronting of a middle-high vowel by a high, that is, less vocalic and thus nearly consonantal vowel. The phonological difference between /ie/ and /je/ is, in fact, gradual in that the step from the high (most obstructive) vowel /i/ to the semi-vowel /j/, with its relatively low degree of consonantal obstruction, is minimal.

The way in which the different types of phonetic variation 'co-operate' can nicely be seen in the entry ALE-HOUSE (in Figure 8.8), which we may use to sum up. Figure 8.8 zooms the entry in close-up.

In Figure 8.8, we have *h*-dropping (*us* for *house*) side by side with *j*-insertion and diphthongisation, which have both affected the pronunciation of *ale*. Interestingly enough, there is no evidence of *h*-insertion here *(*hale)*, which may warn us not to overestimate its importance. The sum total for *h*-insertion with word-initial a*, merely twenty-six items, suggests that hyper-correction by inserted *h*, though quite an issue in the twentieth century, was still a relatively marginal aspect of dialect speech in the nineteenth.

---

[9] There are twenty-three matches for *a** changed to *ya**, eighty-two cases of *e** > *ye** and ten cases of *o** > *yo**, but only one sample of a *yi**-variant for *i** and of *yu** for *u**. Obviously, the propensity of inserting a consonant is stronger when the vowels concerned are on the sonorous side (i.e. low or mid-tongue).

8.3.2   Parts of Speech: Pronouns

Parts of speech is one of the simpler filters. Their relation or affinity to dialect speech seems to be a fairly new field of research (cf. Markus 2014, on interjections). It stands to reason that the language of dialect, that is the language of common people, is in some sense more 'basic' (though not more primitive), that is, educationally less elaborate in the manifestation of its systemic potential that English generally has due to its historical hybridity as well as, in the more recent centuries, by its internationality. In more concrete terms, the impulses of language change that affected the British Isles in their history certainly did not reach all native speakers, including dialect speakers, alike. If this is true in principle, it will result in relative frequencies of certain types of words in comparison with their relevance in the English Standard. Apart from interjections, it may be assumed that particles, adjectives, in particular participial adjectives, and adverbs are good candidates for statistically deviant frequencies in dialect.

Wright has also lemmatised some common phrases so that the *part of speech* of these entries is 'phr.'. By and large, the number of such lemmatised phrases in *EDD Online* is limited. They can all be found via the filter *parts of speech*. Many more phrases are, however, included somewhere in the entries, usually following the marker 'Also in phr.' Moreover, there are further phrases in the blocks of *citations* as quoted from sources. These two kinds of covert phrases can be grasped via the parameter *phrases*.

The informative value of all these types may not be the same, but if scholars have easy access to all of them, they have a good basis of material to start from. They may search for constituents of phrases, for example, phrases with 'as/like' for tracing comparisons, or with *and*, for tracing binomials. Or they may focus on the internal structure of phrasal verbs and composite predicates (cf. Brinton and Akimoto 1999), investigating the role of semantically 'weak' verbs such as *to go, to do, to make*, and perhaps also including sonorous patterns of phrases (alliteration, assonance, consonance, rhyme).

One part of speech that I have found very promising from the viewpoint of dialect is that of pronouns. As function words, they are, of course, high-frequency words and particularly subject to dialectal impact. It, therefore, seems worthwhile taking a closer look at them in *EDD Online*.

In the *EDD* most of the 163 items of pronouns are simply marked as 'pron.', but eight of the personal pronouns are identified as 'pers. pron.', thirty-one of the demonstrative pronouns as 'dem. pron.', and there are also a few

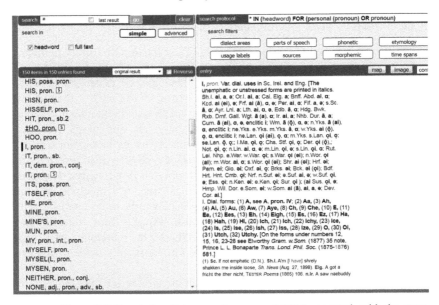

Figure 8.9 Search for all 'personal pronouns' OR 'pronouns', with the entry for the first-person singular pronoun opened

specially marked possessive, relative and reflexive pronouns. Demonstratives and possessives are also sometimes called 'dem./poss. adjectives'.[10]

Researchers working with *EDD Online* may react to these inconsistencies of the *EDD* in marking pronouns by searching for the specific type of pronoun they may have in mind, for example, *personal pronouns*, and by adding the general part-of-speech category 'pronoun'. They then have to put in some manual work when selecting the personal pronouns from the list of headwords simply marked as 'pron.'. Figure 8.9 provides an idea of what the task in question is.

Figure 8.9 illustrates the considerable wealth of forms, both in terms of different entries and in terms of the phonetic variation of a particular head-word – note a large number of variants in the right half. We can also see that the form selected in Figure 8.9, the first-person sg. *I*, is simply marked as a 'pron.', so that it would have escaped in a search for 'pers. pron.'. This, in fact,

---

[10] For the sake of completeness, mention should also be made of the thirty items of 'indef'. in a full text query. Most of them are identified as pronouns or articles, but some of them are called 'adjectives'. Some cases of 'indef.' and many other passages with 'indefinite*' have semantically defining functions. We have left out the indefinites in the options provided as *parts of speech* for merely practical reasons – the disentanglement of the different forms and functions for the other pronouns was labour-intensive enough.

holds true for the second and (partly) third person singular as well. HE occurs twice, as a 'pron.' and as a 'pers. pron.'. SHE is marked as a pronoun and a substantive, whereas YOU is marked as a pronoun as well as an adjective and a verb. Multifunctionality of words in terms of word types – morphologically speaking, zero-derivation (cf. Kastovsky 1968 u.ö.) – is, of course, also a common phenomenon in the Standard variety of English. It seems, however, particularly typical of dialectal language. In addition to the formal abundance, we are, thus, confronted with the functional multiplicity of dialectal forms.

To prove this type of complexity of dialectal speech would go beyond what this sub-section on parts of speech can provide. 'Dialect' as such is, of course, a theoretical construct, a super-system composed of singular sub-systems. No specific Late Modern English dialect owns all the forms that *EDD Online* provides for, say, the second person of the personal pronoun. Nevertheless, it is most fascinating to discover which different forms and functions occur for the Standard form *you*, even if they do not belong to an identifiable group of dialect speakers.

The forms that can be assembled from the match list of Figure 8.9 are THEE, THEEST, THOU, YE, YEES, YOU, and YOUS (2×). THEE, THOU, YE and YOU are based on the well-known historical forms for the second person, marked for case and number respectively. Therefore, our first conclusion is that the old forms have surprisingly survived in dialect well into the Late Modern English period. Our second conclusion is that even YOU, like the other word forms, appears in a large number of variants. Figure 8.10 gives us the entry for YOU as an example.

The dialectal forms in Figure 8.10 allow for several conclusions. To highlight one point, the forms show a phonological reduction in weak positions by either deleting the initial consonantal element /j/ or, more often, by reducing the vocalic element, sometimes even to zero (in number 13). The features [length] and [rounded] are also involved in the list of variants, to which we may add the shorter list of phonetic transcriptions. The role or lack of emphasis certainly comes into play in the formation of the variants as well, but the exact *raison d'être* of all these forms has to be the issue for further detailed studies, as the usages of YOU in phrasal contexts.

The same holds true for THOU. Being the original singular nominative form, the bias to vary under the impact of frequent use is even more striking than in the case of YOU. THOU has forty-seven variants listed, and particularly many contracted forms, such as *tusdoon* for 'thou hast done'.

However, the more interesting cases are those with suffixal –s or –st: THEEST, YEES, and YOUS (2×). THEEST, in the context 'Theest talk of silling' sheers', shows anticipation of the verbal suffix by its being added prematurely to the pronoun. The form is identified as Cornish and also attested in the variant form *thees*, which, however, seems to be simply based on

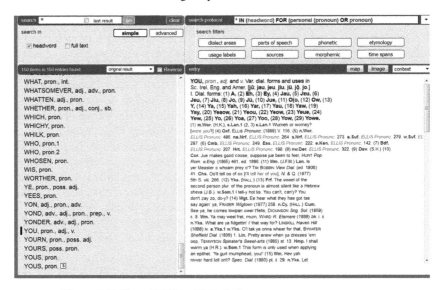

Figure 8.10 Entry YOU in *EDD Online*

phonologically motivated cluster reduction. The addition of a verbal suffix, here for the second person singular, to a pronoun is, of course, against all grammatical rules. With all its rarity, this kind of 'ungrammaticalness' is not uniquely limited to (Cornish) English. In Austrian dialects, for example, Tyrolean, one can hear parallel constructions with an *-st* prematurely and redundantly suffixed to a pronoun: *wannst willst* (for *wenn du willst, 'if you will'*).[11]

The forms YEES and YOUS are, unlike *thees*, not based on cluster reduction, but show a secondary plural suffix, although the two underlying forms *yee* and *you* are original plural forms. Since *you* had lost its former plural function, dialect speakers marked its plurality when needed by an additional suffix. YEES is decidedly Irish. YOUS is likewise attested to Ireland, but also to America and Australia. As regards the motivation for these forms, it could well be that people overseas were less aware of the original plural function of YOU, or, maybe less under the impact of British eighteenth-century language indoctrination.

The restriction of YOUS to dialect areas overseas does, however, not stand up to a closer examination. The *EDD Supplement* has added evidence of

---

[11] Christian Mair (Freiburg), a Tyrolean by birth and an inhabitant of Tyrol in his younger years, kindly brought this idiosyncrasy in the Tyrolean dialect to my attention in the 1980s (spoken communication).

YOUS in Norfolk, though with only one quotation. But the example shows that the re-analysis of the YOU-form as a singular and the ensuing formation of a new plural were not limited to overseas varieties.[12]

Our excursion into the formal and functional productivity in the field of personal pronouns was just one example of the many issues that could be raised on pronouns. Concluding this section, one should underline two aspects that have been tackled earlier but that I could not elaborate on: one is the role of [+- emphasis] for the phonetic manifestation of pronouns and, thus, for their abundant variation. The other is the enormous role of contractions and clitical forms in the domain of pronouns: *ivtle* stands for 'if thou wilt', *tusdoon* for 'thou hast done', etc.[13]

8.3.3   Phonetics: Search for [χ] and [sk]

The filter *phonetic* has a threefold purpose. First, it provides a keyboard of special characters, arranged linewise as 'semi-allographs' of the cardinal vowels, so that <a> subsumes <æ>, <ā>, and so on, whereas the consonants and the raised dot (for stress marking in phonetic transcriptions) are less frequent and, therefore, all provided in just one line at the end. This first option of the keyboard allows for users to search for any string with a special character in it within any parameter of the *simple* or *advanced* mode, for example, in *headwords*. Second, users may be interested in the phonetic transcriptions of headwords, which is, of course, not the same thing as their spelling. This second option is on offer for detailed phonological and phonotactic investigations in dialect speech, for example, in view of processes of assimilation, or of what Wright, as had done many before him, often referred to as 'corruption' (also cf. the filter *usage label*/sub-filter *phonology* on such issues). Finally, there is a third option, covering phonetic transcriptions also outside the reference frame of the headwords. Unbracketed pseudo-phonetic spellings, as were generally common in the nineteenth century, are excluded here. Such unmarked spellings of phonetic relevance are only included in the search routine of *full text* (the button next to the *headword* button in the 'simple' search mode).

The search for *phonetic* data in *full text*, no matter which of the two types mentioned, does not allow for a combination with other filters because *full text* structurally is a rather mixed bag and because the definition of a pre-API

---

[12] According to Kortmann (2008: 487), *Yous* or similar forms can nowadays be found in IrE, ScE and Tyneside English, as well as in 'other areas in the North heavily influenced by Irish immigrants, such as Liverpool and inner-city Manchester'. This shows the post-*EDD* socio-linguistic dynamics of originally area-specific forms.

[13] None of the points raised in this section has been tackled by Kortmann (2008) in his summary on pronouns (pp. 486–8).

phonetic transcription versus pseudo-phonetic spellings is bound to be fuzzy. The restrictions on *full-text* queries concerning phonetics in combination with other filters, therefore, make sense.

There are no such restrictions for searches in the *phonetic-transcription-of-headwords* mode. It freely allows being combined with other filters, such as dialects. It is, therefore possible to trace the areal distribution of, say, words with word-initial [sk*]. This would be a search based on the assumption that such words are likely to be of Scandinavian origin.

A minor disadvantage of our phonetic search engine, however, is that Wright has often listed transcriptions of a headword summarily, without giving a clear reference to dialect areas. The headword CROON, for example, has nine variants, which are dialectally identified, but the bracketed transcriptions [krūn, krun, krün, krœ̃n.] can only be correlated to both the variant forms and the given dialectal areas by the historically trained linguist. Our software, in a search for rounded /ü/, retrieves the transcription [krün], but then attributes all dialectal areas of the headword CROON rather than of the specific [ü]-transcription. Unfortunately, this lack of precision even concerns passages where Wright has, by exception, unequivocally marked transcriptions by dialectal areas.

In the face of this drawback of dialect attribution to phonetic transcriptions, we have equipped the button triggering phonetic transcriptions of headwords with a warning note (in red). The warning is pointless as long as there is only one transcription given to a headword. In the rarer cases where two or more transcriptions are provided the correlation to dialectal areas is subject to the user's insightful philological interpretation.

To illustrate the risks of the phonetic filter with an example, Figure 8.11 shows us the results of a query for [χ] as a transcription in *full text*, with the quantification illustrated on a synoptic map.

As Figure 8.11 demonstrates, the move of the cursor to a particular county triggers an additional pop-up window with a zoom of this county and all the figures of interest. In Figure 8.11, I have focused on Lancashire. The numbers in the small zoom box inform us that there have been 317 matches concerning Lancashire in the given query. The relative modes of quantification relate such frequency figures to the overall number of references to the counties concerned. The *EDD* interface in its background has stored the sum totals of references to all the counties – in the case of Lancashire the figure is 7,837. The quotient between the two figures in *per thousand* is 40.4. Lancashire belongs to the 40–49 *per-thousand* group. In terms of colour, this quantity means light green.

However, the data of Figure 8.11, with its distribution of colours on the map, are, to repeat the warning, hardly reliable. Whoever is somewhat familiar with the English language scene knows that the [χ] pronunciation is essentially

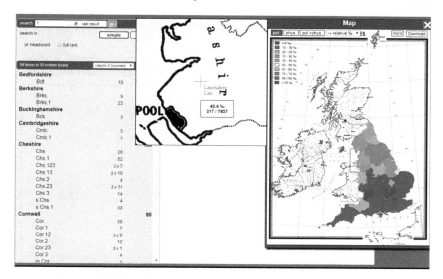

Figure 8.11 Search (in the last result mode) for χ as a *phonetic transcription* in *full text*, with a mapping of the English counties concerned (quantification in *per thousand*)

limited to Scotland and is unlikely to have been distributed all over England in the way suggested by the map in Figure 8.11. The trap one can easily fall into here is that *full text* queries take the text of the *Dictionary's* entries as an unstructured whole. They would, thus, wrongly correlate all English counties found in the retrieved entry to the phoneme at issue simply because it also occurs somewhere in that entry. With phonemes that were generally distributed in English dialects of the LateModE period this global correlation of phonetic pronunciation and dialect areas within the frame of an entry is less problematic. But with [χ], the fairly specific sound of Celtic heritage, the correlation is fatal. Users are, therefore, warned not to carelessly apply *full text* searches in such cases of marginal phonemes.

The less risky alternative for the *phonetic* filter combined with a dialect filter is certainly using it in the option of *headword* reference. Here, only those references to dialect areas are grasped that are in the 'head' (i.e. the first paragraph) of entries. They usually refer to the headword – though not necessarily because they occasionally are related to a specific variant of the headword. In such cases, the relation of the headword to dialect markers is at least an indirect one.

We may check this option with a less marginal phoneme than /χ/, namely word-initial [sk*], which in many words testifies to the significant Scandinavian heritage of English lexis – see Figure 8.12.

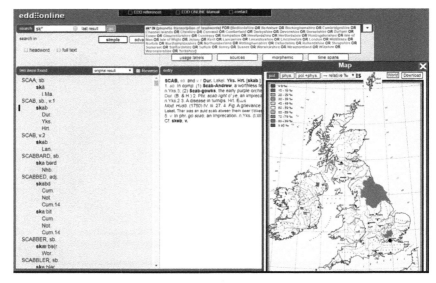

Figure 8.12 Search for *sk** (i.e. word-initially) as part of a phonetic
transcription of headwords (original result)

Figure 8.12 demonstrates the first step of a query for *sk**, with the entry
window of SCAB as a probative example and the correlative map opened. As
we see, *sk**-pronunciation is here represented by <sc> spelling, though there
are also a few cases of <sk> further down in the retrieval list, cut off in
Figure 8.12. The figure shows, in line with our present search, the correct
identification of the three English counties attributed to [skab]. However, in
some cases, Wright has given several phonetic transcriptions in a row, with
different areal targets of reference fuzzily correlated. As an example of this
lack of stringency, we could take the headword SCABBY. The complete entry
looks as follows (Figure 8.13):

It is not exactly clear, and subject to the user's interpretation, which of the
counties highlighted in Figure 8.13 are targeted by the two transcriptions in the
square brackets. While the lack of clarity in this case does not concern our
point at issue (the *sk**-pronunciation), but the stem vowel of SCABBBY, the
example shows that the references to dialects in the context of phonetic
transcriptions are not fully reliable. All we can say is that the phonetic
transcriptions relate to the headword SCABBY.

This conclusion urged us is to give up defining correlations between phonetic transcriptions and dialect attribution. Accordingly, our sorting modes
include the summation of phonetic forms and of dialects, but not their

SCABBY, *adj.* **Nhb. Dur.** Lakel. **Yks. Lan. Chs. Not.**
Lei. Nhp. War. Lon. Dev. Also written **scabie, scaby**
N.Cy.1 **[ska·bi, skæ·bi.]** 1. In *comb.* (1) **Scabby-hands,**
the pig-nut, *Bunium flexuosum;* (2) Scabbed-**head,** the hedge-parsley,
Torilis Anthriscus. (1) **Cum.** (B. & H.) (2) **Chs.1**
2. Of the roof of a coal-mine: rough, uneven, having the
coal adhering to it instead of parting freely from the stone
at the top.
Nhb. But oftener far we had te tew On wi' a nasty scabby reuf,
WILSON *Pitman's Pay* (1843) 33; **Nhb.1 Nhb., Dur.** A seam of
coal is said to have a claggy top when it adheres to the roof, and
is with difficulty separated. It most frequently occurs when the
roof is post or sandstone rock, and is uneven or scabby, GREENWELL
Coal Tr. Gl. (1888) (s.v. Claggy). **w.Yks.** Scabby top (S.J.C.).
3. *Fig.* Dirty, shabby; worthless; mean, stingy.
N.Cy.1 Nhb.1 A scabby fellow. **Lakel.** Noo that's what yan wad
co' rayder scabby. They sarra'd him a scabby turn ower t'toon-lands
(B.K.) **ne.Lan.1, Not.1, Lei.1, Nhp.1, War.3 Lon.** I was the
scabby sheep of the family, MAYHEW *Lond. Labour* (1851) III. 99,
ed. 1861. **nw.Dev.1** A scabby trick.

Figure 8.13 The example SCABBY after search for [sk*] transcriptions

correlation. The only correlation now on offer is that between the phonetic forms and the headwords.

This brings us to the second step of our *sk*-analysis. In Figure 8.14, the sorting mode *column 3 with 1* (rather than *with 2*) provides the 946 headword matches of Figure 8.12 in a 'county-wise' arrangement. The sum total of all county references is 5,889. (For practical reasons, I have limited the query to the counties of England.) The logic behind this quantification is that headwords with an [*sk**]-transcription play the more a role in certain English counties, the greater the reason Wright had to refer to these counties.

The opened entry of SCALE in Figure 8.14 effectively demonstrates that the headword has rightly been subsumed under Berkshire, though the reference to this county is restricted to the variant *scaayle*.

While this presentation step provides information on the individual headwords concerned by our phonetic query of Figure 8.12, a further presentation step (*column 3 counted*) testifies to the quantification of the individual counties, either in absolute figures of occurrence or in relation to all counties activated and, moreover, in relation to the overall frequencies of occurrences of the county references given. We skip over the map showing the absolute figures of occurrence (see Section 6.3.2) and take a look at the more revealing relative percentages (Figure 8.15).

Figure 8.15 visualises the following items: (1) automatic counting of the headwords concerned by phonetic *sk**-transcriptions: 946. (2) automatic counting of the references to counties as tokens and (in bold) as types, with the sum totals, the transfer of the frequency figures onto a map of the UK, and a legend attesting to the value of the colours; (3) the zoom window, which

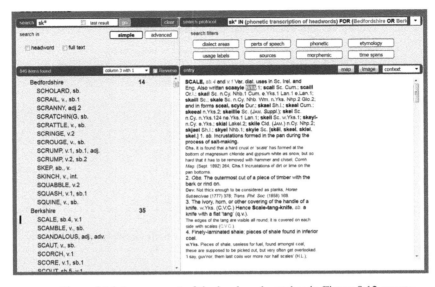

Figure 8.14 Arrangement of the headword matches in Figure 8.12 county-wise (*column 3 with 1*)

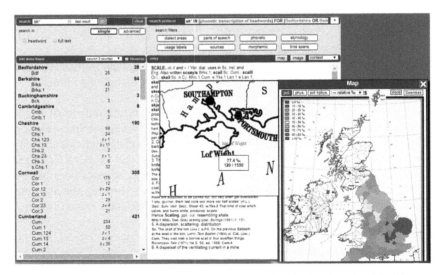

Figure 8.15 Map of relative figures concerning the headwords with *sk**-transcription county-wise

offers further transparency to users, informing them that the red colour refers to the Isle of Wight and is based on 77.4 per-thousand points.

Why the Isle of Wight deviates from the other English counties and has a relatively strong affinity to *sk**-words cannot be argued here.[14] *EDD Online* provides the data for philological or linguistic analyses but does not replace the work of the linguist.

To sum up: the *phonetic* filter is a flexible, yet a tentative tool for investigating phonetic and phonological features of Late Modern English dialects on an empirical basis. Recent scholars, it is true, have compiled such features in didactically helpful surveys (cf. Hughes et al. 2005). But on issues such as the distribution of historical or etymologically informative spellings, rhoticism, the diversity of the stem vowels, and the articulatory reduction of unstressed syllables, including aphetic processes at the beginning of words, *EDD Online* offers itself for higher-resolution pictures than have been available so far from those surveys.

8.3.4   Etymology: *English Dialects and German*

Unlike *phonetic*, *etymology* is a relatively uncomplicated filter. When opened, it allows for two options: the search for special, historically interesting languages, including, in some cases, their previous stages, for example, Old High German. For these options, a menu of the main languages and of their historical stages is available. Note that this menu subsumes very specific etymological references, for example, to the Bremen or Saxony or Cologne dialect in the case of German. The filter scans the whole of the entries, though etymologies are practically always given in the entry-final comments. By default, the filter can be combined with *dialect areas* so that historically interested researchers may try to find correlations between dialect areas (e.g. the South/London/Kent) and etymology (Anglo-Norman/Kentish). It also seems fascinating to trace the correlation of Dutch settlers in East Anglia at the time of the Paston family (fifteenth century) and of Dutch lexical features there in the Late Modern English period. Needless to add that the Scandinavian lexical influence can mainly be located in England's lower north-east more than elsewhere. But given the well-known dexterity of the Viking ships, it is fair to assume (and well-known) that the Scandinavian influx affected not only the England's coastal stripes, including those of the North-West but also parts of Scotland and Ireland, not to mention further European countries.

---

[14] The generally assumed influence of Scandinavian on *sk**-words does not hold true in all cases. French influence also has to be taken into account. Note that the spellings at issue are not only <sc-> and <sk->, but also <squ->. The question cannot exhaustively be discussed here and deserves a study of its own.

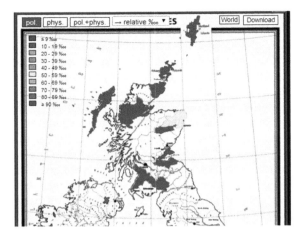

Figure 8.16 Distribution of words with a Viking background in Scotland

Taking this issue as a test case, we will search for all Scandinavian (Danish, Norwegian and Swedish) etymons, including the 'old' and 'middle' phases of these languages, combining the 1712 findings in a second step (*last-result mode*) with all English, Scottish and Irish counties marked. Given the high number of findings, it is advisable to reduce the query at random, for example, to words with the initial letter S. The result (236 items), arranged in the *column 2 counted mode*,[15] shows that the counties concerned in Ireland are, in fact, only coastal ones: Antrim, Donegal, Down and Wexford (48 altogether). For Scotland and Wales we get analogous results, 175 entries with 997 references to the counties of Scotland, 11 entries with 25 references to the counties of Wales. The maps for Scotland and Wales confirm the hypothesis of the primarily coastal impact of the Vikings on the English language. The map for Scotland is given in Figure 8.16.

Why Aberdeenshire is significantly deviant from the other Scottish counties, with the yellow colour standing for only a medium quantity of findings per 10,000 – all the other counties have reached more than 90 points per 10,000 – is one of the issues raised by the map. Answers will have to be found in the future.

This section may be concluded by a short close-up analysis of the word *besom* and its etymological background. *Besom* is a dialectal word for 'broom'.[16] I came across this word when, on one occasion, I was searching for LModE dialect words with some affinity to German. The *EDD* relates it to OE *besma*, MHG *besem* and modern German *Besen*. Having partly grown up

---

[15] This mode, which is difficult for the computer to calculate, is the reason why we need a quantitative restriction.
[16] *Webster's* (1989), with its strong affinity to American English, also has it.

on a farm in the German province of southern Northrhine-Westfalia, I also remember speakers of Low German in the 1950s using the word *besmen*. Checking this word in recent glossaries of Low German, I found the form with word-medial <m> confirmed.[17]

Low German, then, has fairly 'purely' retained the old word for the tool used for sweeping floors, the very word-form that played quite an important role in English dialects. It is true, the word is also included in dictionaries of the English Standard, for example, as mentioned, in Webster's (1989), but it seems to have become marginal in the Standard, with hardly any semantic and no formal ramifications involved. In the dialects, the word is listed five times, with a rich formal variation and derivations added, such as *besom-headed* 'weak-minded, stupid'.

There is no obvious cultural or historical reason why *besom* has lost ground in the Standard variety of English. The basic meaning of *besom* is, as the *EDD* explains, a 'broom, made of birch or heather'. *Webster's* defines *besom* by referring to its usual material of 'brush or twigs'. In either case, one could argue that this is a kind of rougher sweeping implement used on farms in former times (as I again remember from my childhood). While the word *broom,* in its basic meaning, also refers to a plant ('bush with yellow blossoms', Germ. *Ginster*) and, thus, likewise had nothing to do with the synthetic materials mostly used nowadays, it was, at its time and in certain regions, the more efficient tool, due to its finer texture, and thus more adequate to meet with increasing demands of cleanliness. It seems fair to assume that this is one of the reasons why it has finally dominated over *besom*.

Both words owe their meaning of a sweeping tool to metonymy, here a semantic transfer from the material to its function. While *besom* lost ground in the Standard variety of English in favour of *broom*, the two words co-existed nicely in the English dialects of the nineteenth century, with *broom* and *besom* being equally productive (cf. *EDD* entry *broom*). However, the low-German cognate, from which we started on this small excursion, suggests that *besom* is the older word of the two so that its meaning had time enough since West Germanic for a semantic transfer from a type of plant to the implement made of that plant. This is why the *EDD* also testifies to the compound *broom-besom* (*besom* is the determinatum), but there is no combination of the two words with *broom* as determinatum or *besom* as determinant.

To conclude, etymology may give us a clue as to the age of a lexical item and, thereby, help us better understand its semantic development and productivity. *Besom* was more productive than *broom*, also the more productive word in terms of metaphorically derived meanings. One of these attests

---

[17] See www.karl-vom-ebbe.de/suche?id=17&keywords=besmen (accessed 24 March 2019) (Karl vom Ebbe 2017, *Plattdeutsches aus Meinzerzhagen*). The form *besmen* was typical of the south of North Rhine-Westphalia. Further north, e.g. in Frisia, the form *besem* was common.

besom as a 'term of reproach or contempt applied to a woman' (see sb.3). There are, within the altogether seven entries in the *EDD* using *besom*, several derogatory meanings concerning women. Sexism in dialect language is a topic for which *EDD Online* would be a treasure trove. But this is another and too wide-ranging a topic to be tackled in the present context.

8.3.5   Dialect Areas *Combined with Other Filters*

The filter *dialect areas*, unlike the filters mentioned so far, is – in a dialect dictionary – naturally of greater relevance. It can be applied to all query parameters except *full text*, where it would not make sense, as full text implies an unstructured collection of strings. The optional attribution of *dialect areas* to concrete lexemic sub-types, such as *compounds* or *variants*, is one of the main assets of *EDD Online.*

When a search string is fairly specific (for example, the string *house*), the range of filters can be extended all the more. Thus, in the case of *house*, we could ask for all dialectal areas (nations, regions and counties) at a time. In the domain of word formation, to simplify the query routine, one may opt for the parameters *compounds, combinations* and *derivations* simultaneously, as they are rather similar in the way Wright refers to them in the entries.[18]

There is an enormous quantity of dialect filters: 145 counties, 43 regions, and 13 nations, with the counties additionally compatible with the four degrees of precision (*precise, part, fuzzy* and *directions*). Arithmetically speaking, the number of options thus offered amounts to no less 636. Moreover, several counties, regions and nations can be searched for simultaneously with the Boolean operators OR or AND as well as with the marker ONLY. To avoid overburdening our server, the *select-all* buttons switch off both the AND operator and the ONLY function.

The complexity of the search routine is increased by the fact that the filter *dialect areas* can generally be combined with the *labels*, and, in the cases of *compounds/combinations*, *derivations* and *phrases*, with the filter *time spans*. It is, thus, possible to search for phrases from a certain county which have pragmatic implications and have been attested in a certain time. It is also possible to combine the filter *dialect areas* with that of *sources*.

To test this ambitious toolbox of the dialects in their interrelation with other linguistic items and with the history of English, we will, in the following, study the dialectal orientation of the ME so-called *Gawain* works.

The four Middle English works in MS Cotton Nero A.x. were written in the same hand and, allegedly, in the same dialect. This is only one reason among

---

[18] They, accordingly, got the same tag in our XML text, namely *re* (for *reference*) plus the specific attributes COMP, COMB and DERIV respectively.

others, and not a cogent one, why *Sir Gawain and the Green Knight, Pearl, Cleannesse* (or *Purity*) *and Patience* have commonly been attributed to one and the same anonymous author of the West Midlands, the so-called *Gawain* (or *Pearl*) author (cf. Howard and Zacher 1968: IX–XI). They can now be analysed in view of their dialectal lexis by extrapolating from the status of the English language as represented by the *EDD*.

The *Gawain* works are, as is well known, fairly unequal from a literary point of view. *Sir Gawain* is an Arthurian romance in alliterative long lines plus shorter end rhyme lines. *Pearl* is, basically, a Christian allegory and vision of the Celestial New Jerusalem. *Purity* is a homily related to the virtue addressed in the title, with various exempla from the Bible. And *Patience* is a popularised version of the Book of Jonah in the Old Testament.[19] Despite these generic differences, many critics have assumed that the four works are by one poet. The arguments have mainly been based on the poetic qualities of the works (as in Davenport 1978; Markus 1971), rather than on criteria of the unique B. L. Cotton Nero manuscript or on features of language. The common authorship has, however, never been proved. Spearing is one of those critics who do not exclude the possibility that 'the poems were the work not of a single poet but of a school of poets' (1976: 40). This chapter does not suggest to argue on points of literature, but linguistically, returning to the old issue of what dialectal lexis the four works use.

Since the very beginning of their editorial history, the *Gawain* works have been difficult to attribute to a certain dialectal area. As said Morris (1864: xxiv f.):

But although we may not be able to fix, with certainty, upon any one county in particular, the fact of the present poems being composed in the West-Midland dialect cannot be denied.

Similarly, Davis (1968: xxvii) demonstrated that 'The language [of *Sir Gawain*] is not a simple and self-consistent dialect', but 'no doubt, as most scholars have long believed, a dialect of the north-west Midlands'. He also names two words in the vocabulary of *Sir Gawain* that are in modern times testified to in specific dialect areas, *kay* and *misy*. The one is recorded only in Lancashire and Cheshire, the other only in south Lancashire. However, Davis adds that 'survival in dialects is erratic and an unsafe guide to fourteenth-century conditions' (xxvii). Howard and Zacher (1968: X) are similarly agnostic, concluding their discussion of the dialect issue by the complaint that '(the) dialect (of *Sir Gawain*) is terribly difficult' and that the learned author's literary language 'borrowed words from other dialects' (1968: X).

---

[19] *St. Erkenwald*, a fifth work included in Cotton Nero A.x., has occasionally also been seen as a candidate for having been written by the *Gawain* author, but most critics have not shared this opinion (cf. Benson 1965). The work is not even mentioned in the *EDD*.

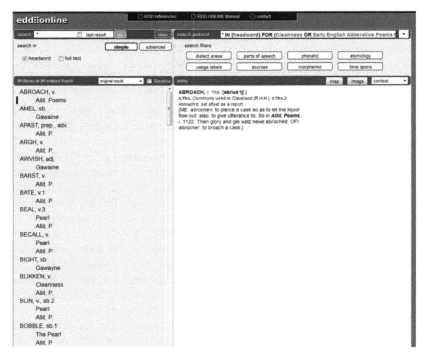

Figure 8.17 Beginning of retrieval list after search for headwords associated with the four *Gawain* works

This study questions the opinion that the survival of former English dialect words should be of so little relevance to their areal distribution, on condition that this distribution can thoroughly be analysed and does not have to rely on eclectic examples. I will analyse the number of words surviving from the *Gawain* works in Late Modern English dialects, moreover, the form (in terms of word formation), place and time of these survivals. The evidence will be based on statistics. It relies on dialect words of old being more persistent and perennial than one would perhaps assume from a twenty-first-century point of view.

Figure 8.17 shows us the first twelve of ninety-six headwords of a match-list, with the first one on the list opened. The first five examples of the list may be taken as test cases for finding out what the *EDD* information is worth in view of the relation to the *Gawain* works.[20]

---

[20] The complete list is planned to be dealt with in a separate paper in the future.

The first headword ABROACH is quoted from the collective edition *Alliterative Poems* (Morris 1864) for its specific (metaphorical) meaning 'to give utterance to'. The dialectal use in North Yorkshire is associated with the past participle form *abroach'd*. This weak form of the participle, again with the non-literal meaning ('set afloat as a report'), is then testified to in one of the *Gawain* works, as against the strong form *abrochen*, given for ME in general. The concept of 'abroaching a cask', obviously at the root of the metaphorical meanings, was also known in Chaucer's Middle English (cf. Stratmann 1891 [repr. Bradley 1968], *abroche*). The example shows that the connection of the headword with the *Gawain* works was, formally and semantically, specific: the participle survived in its weak form and in its metaphorical meaning.

The second entry in our list of Figure 8.17, AMEL, is an aphaeresis of *enamel* and, in this reduced form, localised in Scotland (thanks to Jamieson). The evidence from *Sir Gawain* shows merely formal variation. APAST, the next match, is spatially attributed to six English counties and, in the form *apassed*, traceable both in Chaucer and the *Alliterative Poems*. These first three headwords are all etymologically based on French.

This is not the case in the next two headwords, which are of Germanic origin. The verb ARGH, localised in Scottish and Lincolnshire dialect, is again attested in the *Alliterative Poems*. AWVISH, with six English dialectal counties listed, in the form *aluish* occurs in *Sir Gawain*. While, in this case, Wright does not quote the passage at issue in context, he, as usual, gives the exact line of the text.

In sum, the five matches are all valid hits, no matter whether a formal or semantic variation and a French or Germanic or some other etymological background is involved. My perusal of all the other matches of Figure 8.17 has proved that the pattern is always the same: the reference to the *Gawain* works is regularly provided in the final (bracketed) part of the entries and refers to the headword as a whole or some specific meaning of it. The *Gawain* source is always equipped with the approximate date of creation of the original manuscript and with the exact page or line of the word involved. *EDD Online* allows for different sorting modes so that users can focus on whatever aspect of the multi-dimensional results they are interested in. One of the sorting modes presents the number of references to the individual sources after normalisation, as can be seen in Figure 8.18.

According to Figure 8.18, the 96 *Gawain* entries contain 123 explicit references to the *Gawain* works. The two figures not only diverge because some of the entries contain more than one of the five titles or more than one quotation from the same work but also because Wright sometimes quotes *Cleanness, Patience* and *Pearl* from the *Alliterative Poems* so that both titles, of the work and of the edition, co-occur. Taking this double calculation in twenty-seven of the thirty-six cases into account (after a manual checking), the

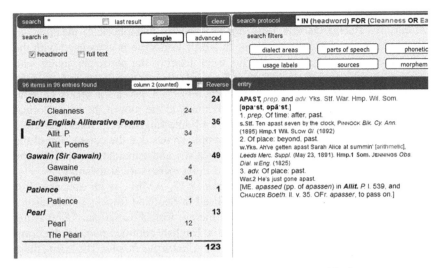

Figure 8.18 Quantification of *Gawain* words work-specifically

number of references to Morris' *Alliterative Poems* shrinks to 9 and the number of the total to 97. For Chaucer, the corresponding number would be 430, for Langland's *Piers Plowman* 192.

Admittedly, the amount of data provided by *EDD Online* for the *Gawain* works is, thus, limited in number, which may mainly be because the works of Cotton Nero A.x were, unlike Chaucer, only discovered in the historicist nineteenth century, with the interest stimulated by Sir Frederik Madden's first edition of *Sir Gawain and the Green Knight* in 1839 (cf. Howard and Zacher 1968: IX–X). From their very beginning in the fourteenth century, the four works were non-mainstream (as it were, 'underground') literature, dug out (and admired) by – in the case of *Sir Gawain* – countless later editors and critics. This is not the place to further discuss the reasons for the initial relative marginality of the *Gawain* works in the history of English literature, but their broad West-Midlands dialect is certainly part of the long neglect.

Wright naturally had no ambition of providing all the words used in the *Gawain* works and still alive in LModE dialects. However, one of the assets of *EDD Online* is that the nearly 100 words of Figure 8.18 (after the manual control) are at the user's fingertips and that they can easily be referenced to other ME works, such as *The Wars of Alexander* and *Morte Arthure*, which have occasionally been affiliated with the *Gawain* author (cf. Gollancz 1940: XIII; Morris 1864: IX). Even so, words are not the 'whole story' and a hardly sufficient criterion for judging on the common authorship of different works. In their migratory behaviour, it is true, words are erratic and 'opportunistic'.

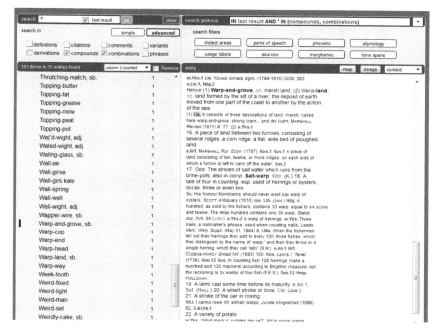

Figure 8.19 Extract of query results for *compounds* and *combinations* after the previous search for *Gawain* headwords (the *last result* paired with *column 2 counted* sorting mode)

This may be less the case if words are grammatically integrated – in terms of syntax or word formation. In the *Gawain* example above, it is striking that the verb ABROACH did not survive as such, but in the form of the (weak) participle. It also seems worth now taking a look at combined lexemes – derivations, compounds, combinations – and at phrases. The 97 entries correlated with the *Gawain* works contain 98 derivations, such as *warpling* (from WARP),[21] 151 compounds and combinations, such as *boose-cheese* ('cheese made before the cows are turned out to grass in the spring'), and 66 phrases, such as *plain and plat* ('clear, distinct'). These overall 315 lexemes and phrases add up to the 97 headwords first retrieved as *Gawain* survivals. Figure 8.19 shows us the results of a specific search for *Gawain*-compounds and -combinations.

Figure 8.19, in this specific arrangement of the matches *qua* alphabetised compounds/combinations (*column 2 counted*), demonstrates the relative productivity of *warp* (and also of *weird*) in post-ME dialect lexis.

---

[21] A *warpling* is 'a calf born before its time' (prematurely 'thrown out', as it were).

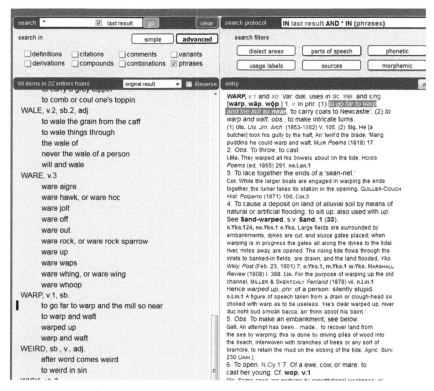

Figure 8.20 Search for phrases in the *last-result* mode, with preceding filter *Gawain works*

This *column 2* presentation (in Figure 8.19), which also implies quantification, will be of less interest in the case of searches for *phrases* – here the default order of listing them under their headwords, functioning as keywords, is more appropriate. In this mode of presentation, the phrases are held together by their arrangement under the headwords concerned – as can be seen in Figure 8.20.

The exact meaning of the sixty-six retrieved phrases in Figure 8.20 is of little concern in the present context. They all testify to the survival of words that lost ground in LModE standard and – like rare species in nature – found their 'habitat' in very specific dialectal contexts and 'cotexts'. The 'cotext' (a text-linguistic term for their syntagmatically being embedded) has manifested itself in the large number of phrases, often of a proverbial kind, as in *to go to warp and the mill so near* or *after word comes weird*. The dialectal context is specific in that the phrases concerned seem to have survived mainly

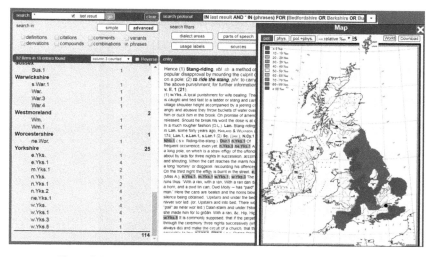

Figure 8.21 Rearrangement of the results of Figure 8.20 for phrases according to the dialectal areas concerned (after a *last-result* search)

in remote dialectal areas, such as Uls. (Ulster), Slg. (Sligo), I.Ma. (the Isle of Man), and Cor. (Cornwall). However, whether this first impression generally holds true, remains to be seen (cf. below). In any case, the marginal position of the *Gawain* words in the fourteenth century persisted in diverse ways of marginality. These words were not only locally and syntagmatically marginalised but also paradigmatically. For the paradigmatic usage, the verb *beware* may serve as a good example. Aphetically clipped to *ware*, it was used in several phrases for warning somebody in a specific everyday context –which is suggested by the results selected in Figure 8.21.

Figure 8.21 illustrates the role of phrases for the issue of lexical survival, in addition to that of monemes and composite lexemes. The sum total of phrases, given at the end of the list, is 114. At the same time, we can see the mechanism of counting in the *last-result* mode and the functioning of the different sorting modes. The areal distribution of the 114 phrases can best be visualised in the *column 3 counted* mode, as illustrated in Figure 8.21. The pop-up map shows that there are three groups. First, we have the North-East, with the exception of Lancashire and Westmoreland. Second, Devonshire, Berkshire and the Isle of Wight likewise have more *Gawain*-phrases in their repertoire, twice as many as the lilac areas on the map. The third group comprises tendentially urban areas between Nottinghamshire and Dorsetshire and – surprisingly – Cornwall.

The question that now seems of interest is whether the maps for composite words and monemes are similar in their dialectal distribution. One would

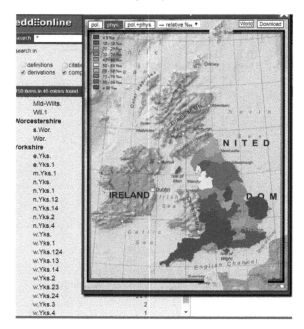

Figure 8.22 Map (per 10,000) illustrating the distribution of 339 derivations, compounds and combinations with *Gawain* background

assume that they both are, on average, less long-established than (idiomatic) phrases. But this is speculation. Here are the facts, revealed by the – this time, physical – maps (Figures 8.22 and 8.23).

There is more variation now than in the map for phrases (cf. Figure 8.21), yet with a clear tendency to the higher frequency figures north of the line from Lincolnshire to Cheshire. In Figure 8.23, based on the frequency numbers for monemes, this clearer picture is further focused. The 2,776 references to English counties predominate in the northern Midlands and the North.

On the map of Figure 8.23, the area where *Gawain* words fell on fertile ground and have survived well into the LModE period is distinguishable from the rest of England. Again Nottinghamshire is an exception, but otherwise the line from Cheshire eastward to the Wash is plainly discernable, with the colours turquois, light- and dark-green dominating the picture. Note that the map of Figure 8.23 is based on figures *per thousand*, whereas in Figures 8.21 and 8.22 we have referenced the matches to 10,000. If one likewise used this measure for the moneme results, the uniformity in the South would fall apart and show considerable differences of *Gawain*-reception there. This simply shows that the scale of a map is like glasses, deciding about what we can see.

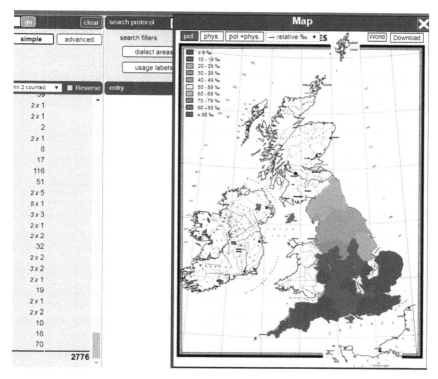

Figure 8.23 Search for monemes with *Gawain*-background plus map (per thousand)

In sum, when tackling the question of lexical survival, one has to take into account not only monemic words but also composite lexemes and phrases, the more so since words coming in idiomatic phrases could survive the more easily. The question of where the survival predominates, however, is presented the most clearly in the case of monemes, followed by composite words. Phrases, on the other hand, due to their long-lived persistence, have by and large crossed borders, irrespective of where they were originally coined

8.3.6   *Digging in Syntactic* Usage Labels

The eight types of *usage labels* in *EDD Online* are simply a result of Wright's frequent remarks on usage. We implemented these types mainly during the last phase of the *EDD* project in 2017. A large amount of material is accessible via these labels. The options in phonology, syntax, semantics and pragmatics are

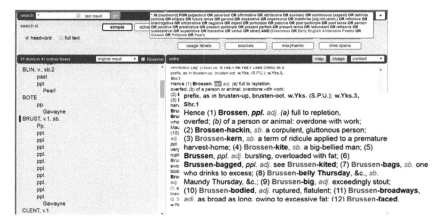

Figure 8.24 Search for syntactically filtered headwords, with cognates in the *Gawain* works (section of result entry BRUST zoomed in for demonstration)

particularly promising. For all of them, there are menus of sub-filter keywords so that users are encouraged to raise new questions. In pragmatics, for example, the dialect language in communication with animals, the jargon of special professional groups, and the language about certain groups of society (women, children, handicapped people) may give rise to innovative issues on the borderline to sociolinguistics and cultural studies. Needless to say, these sub-filters can be combined with each other and with other filters to gain valuable insights. In a recent paper, the focus of which was on the language of corporal punishment I started digging into definitions for 'punishment', 'beat*' and the like, and tested their affinity to specific groups of people (e.g. boys, teachers) or institutions (schools, etc.) by adding the pragmatic sub-filters concerned (Markus 2019b). The combination could be achieved via the *last result* button, described and applied earlier (see Sections 6.2.2 and 8.3.5).

One of the sub-filters provided by the *usage labels* is *syntax*. It concerns a linguistic domain often topicalised in recent dialectology.[22] The possibility of combining issues of syntax with selective filters of sources adds an extra dimension to researchers' investigations of historical syntactic continuity and change. Figure 8.24 presents a concurrent query for all syntactic features grasped by Wright, filtered by the criterion (borrowed from the last sub-chapter) 'source = *Gawain* works'.

For the user to see the complexity of the query, I have smart-tagged the search protocol on top of Figure 8.24. The selected entry *BRUST,* with its

---

[22] Cf., for example, the synopsis by Kortmann (2008).

participial form *brossen/brussen* et al., shows, apart from metathesis, that the use of the old strong past participle of the verb *to burst*, testified to in *Sir Gawain* (now invisible at the end of the entry), was still common in nineteenth-century dialect. The participle was, in fact, remarkably productive to form participial adjectives, for example, in compounds with *brossen* or its variants (see the twelve visible examples of such compounds [out of 21] in Figure 8.24). In contrast to dialect, the Standard verb *to burst*, at some stage in the history of English, lost its morphological marker of the past participle form. It is, therefore, no wonder that *burst* as a past participle in the Standard does not share the syntactic flexibility and morphological productivity of dialectal *brossen*, with the examples ranging from *brossen* unspecified (meaning 'overfed') to *brusten up* (meaning 'pulverized'). This use of the participle as a participial adjective (or as part of a noun, see sample [4]: *Brossen-kite*) is just one of many points of evidence that could prompt in-depth investigations. As the retrieval list in Figure 8.24 suggests, plenty of 'syntactic' keywords, with morphological and sometimes semantic implications, are on offer (fifty-eight keywords). The results of the query that Figure 8.24 is based on may be rearranged in the assortment mode according to the syntactic features concerned so that users see at a glimpse which features predominate.

Our navigation in syntactic labels in *EDD Online* has provided some old participial adjectives, as used in the *Gawain works*, still marked by strong inflection. This accidental finding could give rise to a future systematic study of the survival of strong participial forms in English dialects generally.[23]

8.3.7   *Semantics*: Case Study of *Flora* and *Fauna*

When analysing *semantics*, the team members of *EDD Online* found that Latin *termini technici* in flora and fauna are very frequent in the *EDD*. The *Dictionary* contains 6,229 names for flora and 3,377 for fauna. Given these high numbers, we implemented a special tool for searching flora and fauna according to various features. Users get both the Latin names and their Standard English equivalents, so that they may run a query starting from either Latin or English. In addition, users may retrieve the corresponding dialect terms and/or the dialect areas provided for these terms. Thus, they may wish to find out what different dialect terms were in use for daisies or violets, or for the Latin *orchis* ('orchid'), or they may wish to initiate a geography of British bird habitats, following the geography of their names. In Figure 8.25, the result of a query for flora with the string *orchis* as part of its Latin name is presented.

---

[23] Cf. the use in *Sir Gawain* of the weak form of the past participle *abroached*, discussed above in Section 8.3.5.

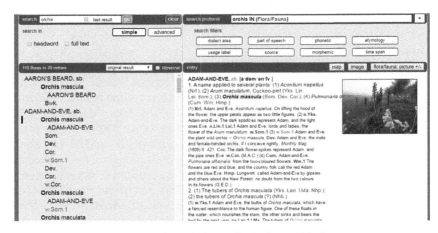

Figure 8.25 Result of search for *orchis* in flora: 114 plant names

As we see in Figure 8.25, *Adam-and-Eve* is one of the dialect names of the *orchis mascula,* with the headword ADAM-AND-EVE (in this case identical with the English name of the plant[24]) and the dialect areas automatically added.[25] We have also implemented links to medial databases (in this case: *Wikimedia*) to prompt pictures of the plant or animal concerned.[26] These links have only been possible for the Latin names – the English Standard or dialect names turned out to be too changeable to be reliable for automatised Internet queries. But even without the pictures interesting questions can now be raised. For example, what terms did dialect speakers use for roses, and what was the distribution of these terms.

In addition to the flora or fauna button, users may wish to activate the semantic label *figurative* to find out what interesting metaphors were coined in the fields of plants or animals. They then have to activate the *last-result* box, adding *figurative* under *usage labels/semantics*. In such *last-result* queries, the retrieval window only displays, in addition to headwords, the items of the second query, in this case, *figurative* or its equivalents (266 matches for flora). But the user can be assured that the headwords listed are a subset of those presented in the first query, that is, the very ones that contained the flora or fauna terms. It is, however, not always the case that the label *figurative* refers to these flora or fauna terms, that is, the headwords – they sometimes refer to a

---

[24] In many other cases, the name of the plant is included somewhere within the entry, e.g. as a compound or phrase. Wright is not consistent in his policy of lemmatisation.

[25] In this search routine, the selection of specific dialect areas via the normal filter of that name is no option.

[26] To avoid copyright problems, we have taken great care to use shareware data only.

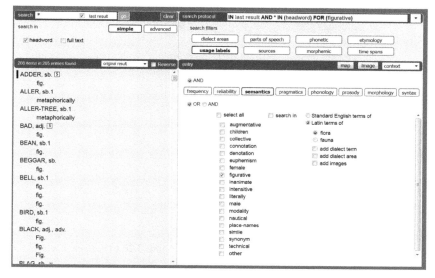

Figure 8.26 Search window for flora- (and fauna-) queries

sub-section of the entry concerned, for example, a compound within the entry. So some manual work, it must be admitted, is left to the user. It seems, however, fair to argue that even so there is still an indirect connection between the marker *figurative* and the headword of the given entry.

To explore the value of the search routine for flora and fauna in *EDD Online*, I recently wrote a short paper on flora (Markus 2017a). One of the results of the paper was that flora terminology testifies to the 'seemingly endless variation of dialectal terms referring to nature' (2017a: 5), with flowers and plants used as examples. The coinages, I found, are often religiously motivated, but also often metaphorical, and occasionally obscenely allusive. The *orchis mascula*, for example, with its suggestive name in Latin, was given English dialect names alluding to the penis, because the tubers or bulbs of this plant resemble testicles – names such as *cock-flowers*, *Johnny-cocks*, and *Priest's pintel/pintle* ('penis') (Markus 2017a: 4f.). In general, the flora terms are mostly a result of people's desire to have 'images of things' (2017a: 5). The *orchis mascula*, highlighted in Figure 8.25, is a good case in point. In its list of findings, forty-eight different dialect terms for this flower show up.

Readers now keen on starting searches for flora or fauna of their own may find it helpful to be offered some assistance on the sophisticated search options available for triggering impressive results. Figure 8.26 demonstrates these options.

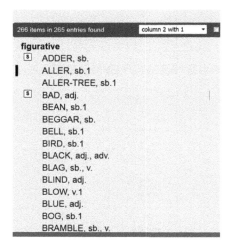

Figure 8.27 Presentation of the results of Figure 8.26 in *column 2 with 1* mode (beginning of the match list)

Figure 8.26 (on the right side of the right half) shows that we have several choices: between the Standard English term and the Latin term; between flora and fauna; and between the three options of what can be added in the retrieval list: the dialect term, the dialect area, and an image of the plant or animal at issue. Moreover, the user can, of course, opt for a specific string or, otherwise, an asterisk. In Figure 8.26, the query has included all flora terms that are affiliated with the marker *fig.* (for 'figurative/metaphorical' etc.). As the headline shows, the query provided an output of 266 items. This list is based on a *last-result* search.[27]

Using these tools and the ever-available implementation of the sorting mode, the results of Figure 8.26 can be re-arranged. Users can either call up the simple list of the flora terms in an A–Z order (Figure 8.27) or they may wish to get the quantified list of the abbreviations/markers used for the figurativeness of the flora terms (Figure 8.28):

Needless to say, Wright certainly did not always mark figurative language use. The same certainly holds true for some of the other semantic features. Even if a query provides remarkably high figures of occurrence, we, therefore, have to reckon with several undiscovered cases.

---

[27] Note that in this mode, which always refers to the headwords of the previous search, the *headword* icon has to be switched on. Also note that the activation of a normal semantic filter (such as *figurative*, in the middle of the column of semantic keywords in Figure 8.26) cannot be directly combined with the flora/fauna queries and is, therefore, switched off automatically as soon as some option in the flora or fauna section is activated.

266 items in 265 entries found	column 2 counted ▾	▣ Revers
figurative		**436**
Fig.	429	
metaphorically	3	
used fig.	4	
		436

Figure 8.28 List of markers used for figurativeness in the context of flora terms (*column 2 counted* mode)

It should, however, be emphasised that the activation of any of the semantic labels, such as *figurative,* altogether annuls the search routine for flora and fauna. As mentioned earlier and as we can see in Figure 8.25, the dialects are, if the icon *add dialect area* is switched on, automatically added. However, this function is not logically compatible with the semantic labels because they sometimes do not refer to the same units of information in an entry as the dialect markers. Given this risk of misleading information, we have, after initial attempts, cancelled the option of a direct combination. In other words, the two halves of the filter *usage labels/semantics* have been programmed to be mutually exclusive. The only way to combine searches for flora or fauna with semantic sub-filters is *via* the *last-result* mode, as practiced in the query of Figure 8.26.

8.3.8   Sources: The Ubiquity of Shakespeare

As mentioned earlier, our work soon revealed that Wright's bibliography of sources was not free from mistakes, gaps, and inconsistencies, for example, in the abbreviations. All the more did we wish to make sure that future research-ers would feel encouraged to trace certain sources of the *EDD* and to pin down mistakes and sources wrongly selected or ignored. Studies of this kind have already been presented (cf. Beal 2010; Cesiri 2010). To prepare our interface for such issues, we have divided the sources into overall four categories, of which the first two are texts of a primarily dialectal and literary interest respectively (*dialectal* versus *literary*). The third group is that of the notes or statements of correspondents (*unprinted*). The correspondents are listed under the heading *unprinted* by their full names, with their initials used in the background. The details of this classification are discussed in Section 6.3.5.

In the following, I would like to demonstrate the possibility of combining filters using 'Shakespeare' as a source – after all, 2016 was a 'Shakespeare year'. There are 468 matches, that is Shakespeare references, in 393 entries. In a previous paper (Markus 2017c), I correlated these entries with time spans,

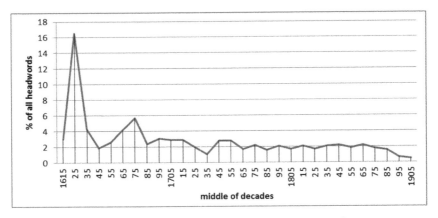

Figure 8.29 Shakespeare words in English dialects across time

segmenting the years from 1600 to 1900 by decades. The result then produced is shown in Figure 8.29.

The curve of the diagram in Figure 8.29, by and large, confirms what would be expected of the reception of Shakespeare's works and the ensuing impact of his language: the strong increase immediately after his death in 1616, the marked decrease shortly afterwards when the Puritans took power and Oliver Cromwell closed the British theatres (1642–1658), the new interest in every-thing theatrical during the Restoration period with King Charles II, the new decrease with the (Protestant) Glorious Revolution in 1688, and finally on to the permanent interest in Shakespeare during the nineteenth century.

However, the spatial distribution is perhaps even more fascinating than the temporal one. Figure 8.30 shows us the distribution of dialect words with an affinity to Shakespeare in the UK.

The map in Figure 8.30 is a 'relative' per-thousand map,[28] that is, the numbers of county references are related to the sum totals of these references and to the numbers of references to each of the counties involved irrespective of sources. While the colours of the map reveal Shakespeare's far-reaching popularity (his 'ubiquity'), the white spots in Ireland, Scotland and Wales are the result of Wright's sparse references to counties there and his favouring larger areas. The distribution in England is not given in concentric circles, with Shakespeare's home-county Warwickshire being the centre, but shows a predominance in the North, the Midlands and the South-West. The East and the South, and London in particular, are clearly less affected by lexical

---

[28] Unlike the one used for the *Gawain* works (in Section 8.3.5), which was based on frequencies of occurrences per 10,000.

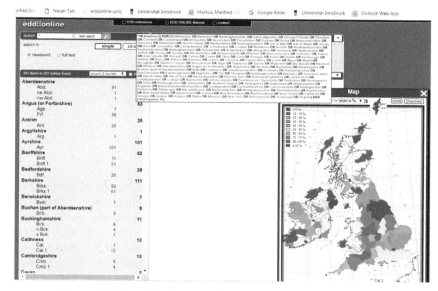

Figure 8.30 Areal distribution of Shakespeare words in the UK (1700–1900)

Shakespeare survivals.[29] Scotland, Wales and Ireland are, overall, poorly represented, with the sole exception of Limerick because of the special role that the poetic genre of the limerick played for Shakespeare.[30]

All in all, however, the map of Figure 8.30 indicates the high integration of Shakespeare's lexis in dialect. It also seems fair to argue the other way around: dialect lexis was an integral part of Shakespeare's vocabulary. His general affinity to 'the people' has often been stated, for example, with a critical undertone, by Alexander Pope, who declared that Shakespeare's audience 'was generally composed of the meaner sort of people' (cf., for the full quotation, Markus 2017c, endnote 2). In more recent times, there have been academic studies of how Shakespeare had an impact on the English language in general, not least in view of idiomatic phrases.[31]

---

[29] Circular patterns in areal distribution have played a dominant role in Göbl's interpretations of his maps. One of the basic rules in his dialectometry is the weakening of a dialectal feature according to the spatial distance from the area where the feature was initiated.

[30] The official initiator of the limerick is, of course, Edward Lear with his *Book of Nonsense* (1846). However, Shakespeare wrote poems that could be seen as predecessors, e.g. in *Othello*, II, 3, also in *King Lear* and *The Tempest* (Legman 1970: xxii, xxxix). Also see Herben (1963).

[31] E.g. Grandage 2016: 1380–7.

9   Focus on Quantification
Towards Dialectometry

9.1   Introduction

In April 2019, the digitised version of the *English Dialect Dictionary* (*EDD Online*) was launched in its new version 3.0, which includes the 179 pages of the *Supplement*, added by Joseph Wright in the last of the six volumes. According to the interface of this all-inclusive version of *EDD Online*, the *Dictionary*, on its 4,600-odd pages, comprises exactly 79,598 headwords, 16,452 compounds, 22,719 combinations, 15,060 phrases, 53,972 variants, as well as references to 202 dialectal areas, 21 parts of speech and 60 etymologically cognate languages. Moreover, it allows for the retrieval of some 4,900 sources and of eight types of usage labels, with overall 150 labels. Needless to add that the *Dictionary* comprises well over 100,000 defining terms and two or three times as many words in the citations, attesting to the points made in the entries.

While *EDD Online* is, thus, a fairly large 'corpus' of dialect-related text, it is also a multifaceted amount of data on which modern quantifying and statistical methods of analysis (such as the chi-square test) cannot simply be applied. However, the imposing numbers just given invite the question of the feasibility of quantification, the more so since various challenging suggestions have been made over the last few years of integrating statistics in corpus linguistics as 'a central component' (Gries 2015: 50; also cf. Rayson 2015: 40–3 on modern methods of retrieval). With a more specific focus on dialects, Orton et al. (1978) (*Linguistic Atlas of England*) and Viereck and Ramisch (1991–1997) developed ways of cartographically illustrating quantities of dialectal distribution. While their emphasis was always on individual dialectal features or a small number of them in comparison, Göbl (1982, 2007) went a step further, initiating 'dialectometry', that is a method of creating radically synoptic maps, based on dozens or hundreds of dialectal features at a time. He mainly applied his approach on Romance languages, but in his wake, various other scholars (e.g. Nerbonne and Kretschmar 2013; Szmrecsanyi 2013; Wegmann 2016) have more recently tried to transfer dialectometry to Anglophone issues, measuring dialectal distribution by abstracting from singular observations in favour of a large-data evaluation, with the aim of visualising such data on maps. In the face of this challenge of quantitative approaches, dialectometry and cartography, there is a need to check the parameters and filters of analysis provided by *EDD Online* in view of the possibility of counting results of retrieval.

9.2   The Versatile Reference of Dialectal Markers

Any user of a dictionary expects the basic principle of order to be the alphabetic arrangement of headwords. 'Headwords' (or lemmas) in the *EDD* are, however, not only words – the entries are occasionally headed by bound morphemes or phrases. This is partly due to the historical character of the *EDD* – it covers the time from 1700 to 1903. Within these 200 odd years, original phrases were sometimes contracted to apparent words, as in the case of *good-bye*, which goes back to the former phrase *God be with you* (or *yee*). A 'word' is, therefore, not a constant unit across time.

Apart from this minor problem concerning the definition of 'headwords', the first question that comes to mind in an English dialect dictionary is, of course, where in the UK or worldwide a dialectal item was used (in the case of the *EDD* we have to add: at some time in the eighteenth and nineteenth centuries). However, another question is equally important, implying a different perspective. It focuses on a specific dialectal area, inquiring what dialectal features can be attributed to it. In the first case, the topic refers to the places of use (the 'habitat') of an item x, and in the second case, we are interested in a particular area y and its items. The two approaches have different repercussions on the quantification of findings. Things seem easy as long as we search for just one specific string, say "HOUSE" (in our first case), and for one specific area, say the county of Bedfordshire (in the second case). Figures 9.1 and 9.2 illustrate these two basic options.

Though the two figures are based on purposefully simple questions, they already show that the *EDD* is a corpus of 'dirty data' (for this term, see Rayson 2015: 33), so that users have to be quite careful about how they raise their questions. In Figure 9.1, the string *'house'*, even if non-truncated, turns out to be polysemous, with four headwords provided, rather than one – the number of findings can be seen above the result list. If we had typed in *house* as a truncated string, i.e. without the quotation marks, there would have been an output of even twenty-six headwords. To avoid such traps, users have to add quotation marks, thus switching off the default truncation, and to activate filters apt to identify the part-of-speech form they have in mind. In the present case of *HOUSE sb.1, v.,* they could, in the filter *Parts of speech*, select *sb. and v.* to find this very form of HOUSE and no other. Furthermore, as Figure 9.1 shows in its entry window on the right, some of the references to counties do

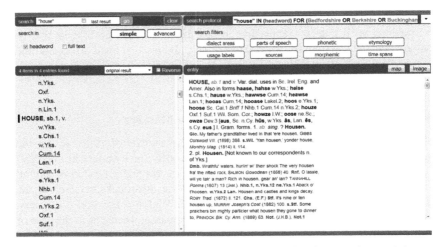

Figure 9.1 Search for "HOUSE" (non-truncated by the quotation marks) as a headword in all counties of the UK (optionally: worldwide)

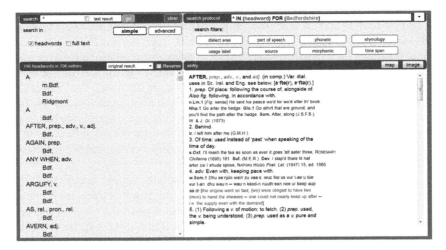

Figure 9.2 Search for all strings (*) from county Bedfordshire

not refer to the lemma *HOUSE* as a whole, but to specific aspects of it, for example, to spelling variants.

In Figure 9.2, the county searched for, Bedfordshire, provides equally fuzzy results: it is also retrieved when only parts of it (m.Bdf., Ridgmont) are concerned. In the face of such imponderable factors, do we have to give up our hope of quantifying result lists from *EDD Online* altogether?

This, in my view, would be a prematurely pessimistic conclusion. However, before proceeding, we should agree on some basic characteristics of observations on dialects.

9.3   Quantification and Normalisation

Dialectology, and English dialectology no less, is an extremely wide field of interest and research. Scholars should, therefore, be clear about what exactly they wish to tackle. In Figure 9.1, the question was that of the geographical distribution of a certain, supposedly dialectal item. Ideally, this item should be unambiguous. Since the string 'house', in Figure 9.1, turned out to be ambiguous, users may simply decide which 'house' they are interested in and consider this case in isolation.

The county references filtered out for the specific item *HOUSE, n. and v.* in Figure 9.1 (or, to be more exact, the visible samples of the list) show up in the confusing original order of the dictionary, also including special directions within counties and strangely numbered references to counties (the numbers are codes marking Wright's sources for these counties). Users keen on quantification would wish to obtain a normalised list of references to counties, with the *differentia specifica*, that is, directions (w.Yks.), partial references (Ridgmont), fuzzy references ('in parts of Bdf.') and source references disregarded as such and counted as normal county references. Along these lines, the results of Figure 9.1 can be rearranged in a quantified and normalised way – as demonstrated in Figure 9.3.

As one can see in Figure 9.3, our software, in *column 2 counted* mode, counts all types of abbreviations of counties including the numbered ones. If an abbreviation has more than one index number (i.e. refers to more than one source), the number of occurrences is accordingly multiplied, as in the case of *Chs.13*, which as such occurs three times, but, given the two sources for Cheshire involved, is counted as '2 × 3', that is, six times. These six references to Cheshire are summed up with the other frequency numbers concerning Cheshire. The full name of this county, rather than any of its shorter forms, is provided as a headline to the abbreviations. The subtotals are listed in the right column and summed up at the end (308 times) – outside the scope of Figure 9.3.

Of course, this method of counting implies simplification. Rather than taking every piece of information on parts of counties at its face values, we are only interested in whole counties.

In my view, this is a sufficiently fine-grained description for survey issues. Subdivisions of counties – in line with small pentagonal areas as distinguished by Goebl and other dialectometrists – would only be needed in the case of issues that focus on special counties. As mentioned, Wright has subdivided

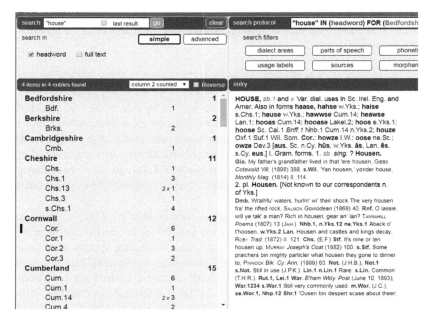

Figure 9.3 Retrieval list after search for headwords with "HOUSE", with quantification and normalisation (*column 2 counted*)

some of his counties, but only eclectically in selected cases, for example, in the cases of Yorkshire and Aberdeenshire. It is for special studies to make use of such information. For the rest, any dialectal analysis includes the question of how specific and fine-grained it should be to make sense.

9.4   Different Types of Frequencies: Entries versus Dialectal References

Another problem involved in simply counting occurrences of special strings, such as the word HOUSE, has to be taken more seriously. The given frequency figures of Figure 9.3 as such are hardly significant, telling us more about Wright's uneven coverage of dialect areas (cf. Praxmarer 2010a) and about his disparate use of specific sources than about the objective relevance of dialect words in these counties. However, given that *house* implies a very general, not to say, universal semantic concept, some other lexical items may prompt more interesting and pointed results (such as *hut* and *cabin*).

In analogy to Figure 9.1, which was based on a search for HOUSE, the results of Figure 9.2, with its search for any strings/words from a selected

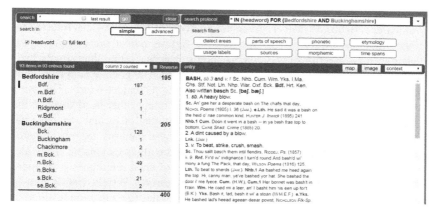

Figure 9.4 Dialect words from Bedfordshire AND Buckinghamshire normalised and counted

dialect area, can also be rearranged in view of quantities of occurrence. To underline the value of this device, Figure 9.4 shows us the results of a query for two counties at a time, Bedfordshire and Buckinghamshire, in this case combined with logical (Boolean) AND (OR and ONLY are also possible and would produce many more and relatively few matches respectively).

Figure 9.4 shows us the selected dialect data for BASH. The total number of entries including references to Bedfordshire (Bdf.) AND Buckinghamshire (Bck.) amounts to 93. However, given that many entries contain several overlaps, the figures for references to the two counties as they have been summed up in Figure 9.4 by far exceed the number of entries involved. There are 195 overlaps for Bdf. and 203 overlaps for Bck. The unequal figures for the two counties are a result of the uneven distribution of the dialect references within entries. For example, one reference to Bdf. paired with three references to Bck. within the same entry is counted as one occurrence, whereas the opposite search for Bck. paired with Bdf. would find the three Bck. occurrences, even though they all refer to one and the same Bdf. token. It is, thus, significant which of the two counties functions as the basis of comparison.

Measuring overlaps also has to be kept separate from the absolute figures of areal references. Seen separately, they would amount to 820 for Bdf. and 688 for Bck. While these figures reflect the intensity of Wright's depiction of the respective counties, the quotas above, concerning overlaps, may be of interest when comparing specific counties with each other for particular reasons. For example, a comparison of Yorkshire with Lancashire would expose what the two counties had in common, notwithstanding their historical animosities. Along these lines, dialect maps could be created as suggested by Praxmarer (2010b). However, given the numbers of Figure 9.4 just referred to, users should be aware of the fact that the figures reflect the complexity of dialect forms – in terms of variants, meanings, usages – rather than simply their occurrence as such. *HOUSE, sb. and v.* has been a good example of this complexity. As a mere word form, it is not even a 'dialect word'. The same could be said of entries such as GO, TAKE and many other headwords in the *EDD*. Their dialectal quality lies in their large number of formal and semantic patterns deviant from Standard English. Since these patterns are most heterogeneous, simply counting them would be methodically questionable. They are, however, quantitatively reflected in the number of areal references – the more often an item is localised, the more dialectal features Wright has obviously found for doing so. There are certainly lemmas in the *EDD* that are testified to with a very narrow 'band' of meaning or usage and for a very small area only, for example, the interjection BAA (Nhb.) and the noun BAALTY-BRAINS (Cor.).[1] But the majority of lemmas, as in the case of HOUSE, are of interest for the sake of their various dialectal features, from the pronunciation of variants to idiomatic phrases with the keyword in them. In other words: for measuring such differences of dialectal productivity and 'dispersion' (Gries 2015), we can at least count the numbers of (various types of) dialectal references (as illustrated in Figure 9.4). Future users of *EDD Online,* it is hoped, will test in detailed investigations what these numbers provided by our counting routine are worth.

Figure 9.4, to be sure, also provides the more basic piece of information: '93 items in 93 entries found'.[2] These numbers are always automatically presented above the retrieval window. The first number (of 'items') refers to what a user has searched for, in our case, headwords. Thus, ninety-three dialectal headwords contain at least one reference to both Bedfordshire and Buckinghamshire.

The difference between such item-figures and the correlative entry figures, on the one hand, and the usually higher figures of references to their dialectal distribution, on the other, may easily give rise to confusion and is, therefore, worth underlining. The item/entry-figures (in Figure 9.4 both 93) mechanically count the number of headwords and entries affected by a certain dialectal (or other) attribution, no matter how relevant, marginal or central/characteristic this item may be for the selected dialectal area(s). By contrast, the counting

---

[1] The ONLY button for isolating such cases, i.e. items that can exclusively be attributed to a certain county, was only recently (2018) implemented. It is one of the functions newly available in *EDD Online 3.0;* for other innovations of this version, see Markus 2019a.

[2] Sometimes entries have listed two or more lemmas so that the figures for items and entries occasionally differ.

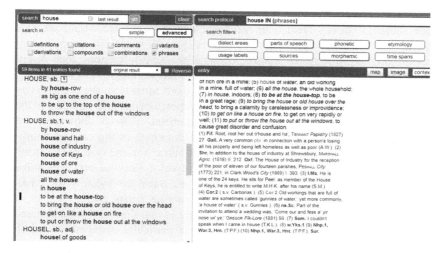

Figure 9.5 Search for *phrases* with the string *house* (beginning of retrieval list)

engine we have implemented in *column 2 counted* mode of Figure 9.3 reflects the dialectal profile of an item. This profile is not only shaped by the (sections of) counties involved, as in our examples of Figure 9.4, but also, in principle, by any of the search parameters, such as *variants*, and filter criteria (such as *time spans*) optionally provided by *EDD Online*.

9.5   Challenge of Statistics in Parameter Searches

Before we come to these filters, this section suggests that we briefly abide by the search parameters on offer in *EDD Online*, beyond the headwords. Figure 9.5 presents the search parameters available in the 'advanced mode'. To demonstrate the possible means of quantifying result lists, we select *phrases* as an example, sticking to the search string used before, HOUSE.

The fifty-nine phrases found within forty-one entries add up to the dialectal profile of the word *house*. Depending on one's interest, one may arrange the matches according to the headwords concerned (*column 1 a-z*) or in an alphabetised list of the phrases themselves (in the white box on top of the retrieval window: *column 2 counted*). Numbers of frequency play a part when we add filters, for example, *dialect areas*. The picture in the retrieval box will be the same as in Figures 9.3 and 9.4. This also holds true for *house*-based *derivations*, *compounds* and *combinations,* which can all be searched for separately or in one go – with the overall result of 310 items in 228 entries.

For lack of space, I abstain from presenting the correlative screenshots. From the statistical survey created in *column 2 with 3* mode, we would see at a glimpse that *bead-house* ('alms-house or religious house'), for example, was more common, due to the number of eight dialectal references, than *beast-house* (another word for *cow-house*, limited to Shropshire).

Beyond such aspects of phraseology and word formation, the productivity and dispersion of the word form *house* (in compositions) is also reflected in the number of formal variants. The search parameter *variants* allows for the retrieval of no less than 1,060 variants in 168 entries in the case of *house-*compositions[3] and another 61 variants (in 11 entries) in the case of the string *house* searched for in the *headword* routine (which likewise produces some compounds and combinations). We can, thus, trace ten variants for ALE-HOUSE ('pub') and sixteen variants for the simplex *house* itself.

The point with all these frequency numbers is that they may be compared with correlative numbers concerning other, in particular, competitive search items. Mention was made above of other terms of the semantic field *house*, such as *hut*, *cabin* and so on. On checking the string *man*, it turns out to be even more productive in English dialects than *house*, but *book* is a relatively unimportant dialect word/string, with only 8 headwords, 15 phrases (in 5 entries), 49 compositions plus derivations, and 129 variants based on it.

Such frequency-based correlations have to be very specific to make sense and for users not to get lost in the data of statistics. Any global quantification seems inadequate. Instead, the specificity should be philologically or linguistically motivated.

9.6   Filter Searches Applied on the Lexical Field of Beverages

One could, for example, trace terms from the lexical fields of drinks such as *tea, coffee, beer, wine, whisky, gin,* and *sherry* (to mention only these) – via the *advanced* button *definitions*. Promising issues would be *tea* versus *coffee*, *beer/ale* versus *wine*, and *whisky, gin* and *sherry* as competitors of each other, with *whisky* typical of Scotland, *gin* typical of the eighteenth century and *sherry* probably most untypical of (lower-class) dialect speakers.[4] Of course, not the

---

[3] This is possible via the *last-result* mode, to be triggered in the search box after a first search for compositions (i.e. compounds, combinations and derivations combined) with *house* and the subsequent search (piggyback search, so to speak) for * (i.e. all items of the previous search), with the button *variants* activated.

[4] To add some provisional evidence for this assumption right away: *sherry* has a *full-text* frequency rate of 6, *gin* as a string occurs 896 times. However, the drink turns out to be a homograph of various other <gin>-spellings so that its exact frequency number cannot be given without a manual analysis. The example shows that *full-text* queries may be of limited value.

drinking habits as such are of interest here, but the repercussions in language structure and usage, along the lines of retrieval that have just been described.

A simple search for '*beer*' as a term of definition provides 241 matches in 222 entries. For '*wine*' the figures are 50 and 49. Now turning on the dialect filter, clicking on *dialect areas*/all English *regions* and (= Boolean OR) all English *counties* (in the *last-result* mode), we get 223 entries for *beer* and 52 entries for *wine*. For Scotland the same queries produce an output of 121 (entries for *beer*) versus 35 (*wine*), for Ireland the correlative figures are 65 versus 20, for Wales 30 versus 7. The share of 'wine terms' in relation to 'beer terms', expressed in rounded percentages, is 22.5 per cent (in England), 32 per cent (Scotland), 32 per cent (Ireland) and 29 per cent (Wales). It is worth noting that these figures do not refer to synonyms of *beer* and *wine* respectively, but to dialect terms semantically or pragmatically connected with them. Though the connection is occasionally loose, we can draw the following conclusions: (1) Dialect terms from the domain of wine generally play only about a fourth of the role of 'beer terms'. (2) England deviates from the rest of the UK by its clearly stronger preference of 'beer terms' (Germanic heritage?), whereas dialect speakers of the UK-countries with a predominantly Celtic background reveal this preference significantly less, with 7–10 percentage points of difference.

Alerted by this example from the domain of drinking, we may now focus our main interest on specific terms of beverages rather than on areas of distribution, thus embracing the more challenging query routines offered by *EDD Online*. For example, on searching for the string *whisky* in the query option of *citations* and activating all dialectal areas at a time (i.e. all *nations*, all *regions* and all *counties* worldwide), the search protocol, which has been opened in Figure 9.6 to be partly visible, is overwhelming. So is the result list with its hierarchical arrangement of headwords, the search word *whisky*, and the dialectal areas concerned. To adapt the retrieval list according to their interests, users may select one of the options in the sorting box, likewise opened in Figure 9.6.

In the present context, the sorting routine *column 2 counted* would be of particular interest. It counts the retrieved tokens of the string *whisky* as part of words and sums them up for the sake of easy quantitative comparison with other search items. Figure 9.7 illustrates this convenient option.

Another mode in the sorting box arranges the findings of the retrieval according to strings (i.e. column 2), with the areas (i.e. column 3) subordinated so that users can easily see where any of the forms shown in Figure 9.6 was used, and how often. The other two modes in the sorting box arrange the data first according to areas (*column 2 with 3*) and then according to word form (*column 3 with 2*). Moreover, these modes count the numbers of word forms for each area listed. Of course, Scotland as a whole and in its parts

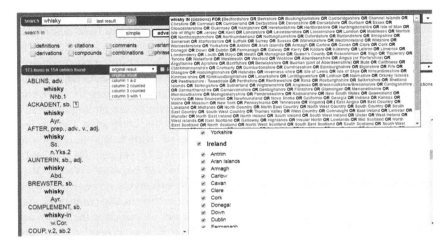

Figure 9.6 Search for *whisky* in *citations,* with the sorting box and the beginning of the protocol box opened

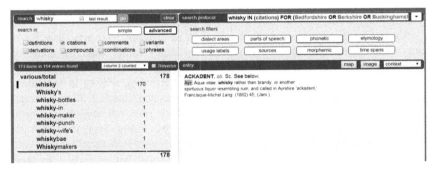

Figure 9.7 Retrieval list of Figure 9.6, with the matches arranged according to strings, and counted

predominates as far as whisky is concerned, followed by northern English counties and Ulster.

In this chapter, the comparison to other beverages mentioned above cannot be carried out to the full for lack of space. Neither is there a need now to complete the picture by searching for the (Irish-American) spelling variant *whiskey* (thirty matches in *citations*). Suffice it to say that *tea* is on top of the ranking list, followed by *beer*, *wine*, *whisky* and *cider* (in this order). *Coffee* has a low rate of twenty-four items in the dictionary's citations. While high frequency in *citations* does not guarantee the same degree of frequency as a proper dialect term – given that the *citations* are a mixture of original dialect words and explanatory text of mainly nineteenth-century authors – we can at least reckon with a certain likelihood of equal frequencies in the *citations* compared to those in other search parameters. To simplify somewhat: if whisky plays a dominant role in citations attributed to Aberdeenshire, there is some likelihood that this is reflected in a high number of dialectal variants, derivations, compounds and/or phrases connected with Aberdeenshire.

9.7   Etymology Revisited and Quantified

Not pursuing the topic of beverages again, we will, to demonstrate method, finally focus on another *EDD Online* filter which invites quantification: etymology. It may, for example, be of interest to find out in which counties of the UK the Flemish and Dutch influence on dialects can be traced most.[5] Marking the sub-filters of the button *etymology* accordingly (I also included *Old* and *Middle Dutch*), the first step is the retrieval of the 340 headwords (in 340 entries), with 382 references to Dutch or Flemish. If we, repeating the same query, then add as filters all *counties* and *regions* available in the sub-menus of *dialect areas,* with the Boolean operator OR switched on, we get a transparent tabloid list of all the areas involved from A-Z, as shown in Figure 9.8.

The retrieval window of Figure 9.8 confirms the earlier observation that the counting mechanism has included 'impure' references to, in this case, counties, such as *nw.Abd.* and *Bnff.1*, and that these particular abbreviations are first counted separately (as tokens) and then jointly with all the other abbreviations of a specific area (as types). The total of the normalised figures, popping up at the end of the area list (outside Figure 9.8) amounts to 8,679 references.

This figure would allow for a valid comparison to other donating languages, such as Scandinavian/Old Norse, Anglo-Norman and so on. Figure 9.8 also underlines the implicit difficulties of counting dialectal observations and the impossibility of counting them mechanically. The entry opened in Figure 9.8, ARGH, is connected with Aberdeen only by its variant form *arrow* and with Dutch only in the Dutch word form *arg*. The connection between these word forms, with their deviant spellings, has only been provided by Wright's expertise – no search engine, unprepared for the task, would be able to 'recognise' this connection.

---

[5] It is well known that Flemish and Dutch immigrants settled in England, Scotland and Wales in considerable quantities as early as the twelfth century and continued to do so during the later Middle and EModE periods (cf. http://blog.nationalarchives.gov.uk/blog/englands-immigrants-1330-1550/; Bense 1924).

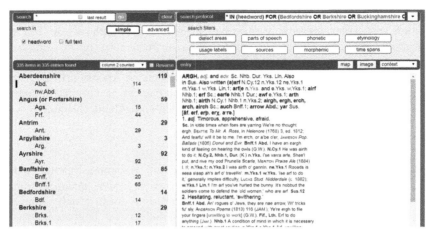

Figure 9.8 Search for all areas worldwide of headwords with Dutch/Flemish cognates, presented in the *column 2 counted* mode

The normalised numbers (in bold) of Figure 9.8 encourage mapping, i.e. the transfer of frequency figures to a UK and world map, respectively. The mapping possibilities of *EDD Online* are the topic of Section 9.8.

9.8   The Mapping of Quantities

The first step of mapping retrieval results in *EDD Online* is by focusing on particular areas concerned by a headword. For example, a search for words beginning with <sc*>, that is, lexical candidates for a Scandinavian heritage, provides the adjective SCABBY, side by side with 822 other such words. A combination with the filter 'all English counties' creates lists of the counties for each of the retrieved headwords. Figure 9.9 shows us a map with the distribution of SCABBY in England, with the red (here: black) colour standing for occurrence, irrespective of frequency.

As the zoom window of Figure 9.9 reveals, users, with the cursor, can focus on an area of their choice to identify its counties. However, this simple function of mapping entry-specific results allows for neither a comparison between headwords nor between counties.

We, therefore, decided for cheropleth maps to be created *ad hoc*, accessible via the button 'quantify' (visible above the map of Figure 9.9). The quantifying maps imply a calculation of frequencies of references to counties under the aspect of the search string (here: <sc*>) and a transfer of these figures to the colours of a map. There are one absolute and three relative modes. The absolute mode simply transfers the type figures of the retrieval list to the pop-

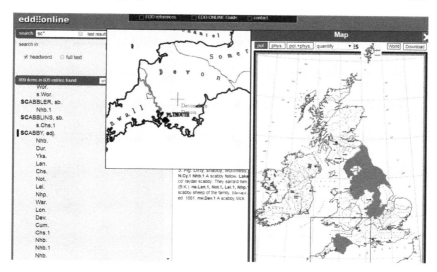

Figure 9.9 Mapping the distribution of a single-entry headword, with a focus on English counties

up map by taking the absolute figures of county references (Devonshire: 351) as a criterion of colour attribution and the sum total of these figures (in our case: 7,275) as a percentage *quorum*. With ten colours standing for 10 percentage points each, from 1 to 100 per cent, the result of this mode of presentation regularly provides little evidence, as usually only two colours are created, one for Yorkshire and the other for all the rest of the counties.

In the more interesting 'relative' modes the result figures of county references are calculated in relation to the figures of all *EDD* references to a given county, first in percentages, then in *per thousand*, and then, for presumably rare items, in relation to 10,000. In the present case of *sc**-words, the best mode proves to be the *per-thousand* presentation (Figure 9.10).

With its fairly good dispersion of colours, the map of Figure 9.10, by and large, allows for the conclusion that the Scandinavian heritage in the form of *sc**-words can be traced most in the counties where one would expect it (given the seafaring competence of the Vikings): north-east of the Danelaw line from the Wash to Chester, and in the coastal counties of Cornwall, Devonshire and the Isle of Wight. Admittedly our picture is not complete without the additional counting of the <sk*>-spellings and word-initial [sk]-transcriptions. The inclusion of these options in the present discussion would, however, lose out of sight the main purpose of this chapter, which is to demonstrate the possibilities of a quantifying analysis.

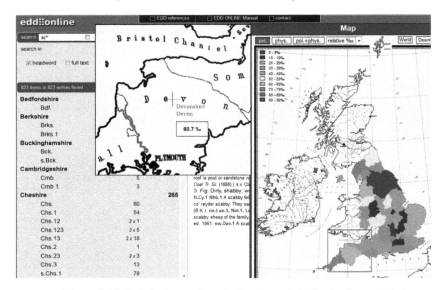

Figure 9.10 'Relative' mapping of all *sc**-words in England, quantified *per thousand*

For the method of quantifying results of *EDD* queries, it is vitally important for a county, region or nation in a special query to have the result figures related to the overall numbers of references to the areas of interest. Only then will Wright's naturally uneven inclusion of areas be corrected.

9.9   Summary and Conclusion: Possibilities of Quantification

This chapter attempted to demonstrate some of the possibilities of quantification provided by *EDD Online 3.0*. I have taken little notice of the equally quantifiable role of the parameter *variants* and of the filter *time span*, to mention only these two. Our focus has been on quantified information concerning dialect areas.

In contrast to the tendency in traditional dialectology towards the observation of isolated items and towards word geography, *EDD Online,* with its now different types of precisely countable data, encourages multi-word or multi-item queries, on the one hand, and multi-areal searches, on the other hand. It is, thus, a suitable tool for describing not only individual dialects and individual dialect areas but dialect *per se* and the typical features of dialect pairs or clusters. The *ad-hoc* production of survey maps is based on normalised frequency figures, with the sum total of occurrences used as a *quorum* for percentage, *per-thousand* (*per mille*) or *per-ten-thousand* ratios. The survey maps put areal units of the users' choice, such as counties, into a perspective. In my view, the individual counties of the UK are a sufficiently large area to be of evidential relevance. As regards the data provided by the *EDD*, there is no need to construct smaller spatial units in the wake of Goebl's pentagons (also cf. Wegmann 2016). Unlike Goebl's dialectometry, we have stuck to a linear representation of quantities, using ten equal spans of frequency and, thus, ten colours. We have not used special statistical formulae to enhance the relevance of our data. We have, however, implemented the three scales just mentioned for measuring the relative weight of output figures rather than their absolute numbers. For most searches, the per-thousand scale will probably be the most useful one.

This does not mean that many of the suggestions forwarded by Goebl and, in his wake, others would be non-inspiring. However, the details of the theory of 'dialectometry' could not be discussed within the framework of this chapter – for a more detailed discussion, see my review of Wegmann 2016 (Markus 2018). The future will show how and to what extent statistical evaluation can be applied to the tables and maps that can be copied and pasted from *EDD Online*.

As part of the initial short demonstration of the search engine of *EDD Online*, Chapter 9 has argued for a multi-faceted concept of dialects, with no specific linguistic field being preferred. There are search routines for all four domains: lexicology, phonology, morphology and syntax. The use of the new Innsbruck platform, therefore, entirely depends on the researcher's motivation and interests. Using the word *house* as an example, we saw that the dialectal character of headwords in a dialect dictionary does not necessarily lie in the word itself, but in the sum of its features: formal, semantic, pragmatic or usage features. It would, therefore, be simplistic always and only to count word forms. The profile of a dialectal form results from its different functions and usages in dialects and finds expression in the number of references to dialectal areas.

One of the functions of the word *house* in dialect has been its role within phrases. We started with an analysis of this word as to its role in dialect, followed by queries on the equally important *house*-based *derivations*, *compounds* and *combinations*. The results have warned us of a mechanical counting of findings. Instead, they suggest targeting keyword groups that are worth a comparison, for example, in the domain of beverages.

Using these as a test case, we were first concerned with the *EDD Online* filters, illustrating the areal distribution of beer-terms versus wine-terms. The comparison allows for interesting conclusions on drinking habits in the UK and on the linguistic repercussions of regional preferences. As a second filter after the dialect areas, I selected the Dutch/Flemish etymological background of dialect headwords, paired with their geographical distribution. This example again shows that the value of the counting mechanism implemented in *EDD Online* not only consists in delivering sum totals of results but also in providing quantitative transparency. We always know what figures refer to.

EDD Online comprises a frightening mass of data at first sight, but confronted with specific sensible questions and due to query results that can be presented in an alphabetised, normalised, quantified and mapped form, it turns out to be an ordered corpus. The complexity of the data is a result of the multidimensional characteristics of English dialects. With the potential of *EDD Online* as regards different search sections, filters and options of display, we may come as close to the confusing features of dialects as is possible at the present time.

10   Final Remarks on the Accessibility and Impact of *EDD Online*

EDD Online can be used by all private persons – researchers, students and amateurs – without charge. All these users have access to our interface without registration and password. They have, however, to accept our copyright and working conditions by a mouseclick before entering *EDD Online*. We will, moreover, automatically count the quota of users, of repetitive use and the like through Google *Analytics*. For this to be possible, users have to add another mouseclick, thus accepting us via Google to statistically register and evaluate the general response to *EDD Online 3.0*. It stands to reason that previous *EDD*-related websites of our Innsbruck-based project will no longer be available online.

I have to add that non-private, i.e. professional users working for profit-oriented institutions and companies get this permission only for the time being in order to be able to test our interface. This is a statement as seen from March 2019. It is, to put it frankly, not clear yet whether firms will be granted this license for good. The answer to this question depends on whether further Austrian funding will be available to the *EDD Online* project in Innsbruck in the near future. Some, though not a large amount of money, will probably be needed for revisions of *EDD Online* and for keeping our server smoothly running. Needless to say that a voluntary donation for this purpose would always be welcome.

I hope that *EDD Online* has an inspiring effect and encourages imitation in the sense that other dialect dictionaries or glossaries are going to be analysed and digitised similarly, including those of present-day German dialects. Even more do I hope that dialectology as an academic linguistic discipline may profit from the approach here presented and moves away from dialectology old style, with its local distribution of old words in the centre of interest. We certainly have to start from the local and temporal distribution of lexis. But linguistics can add much, driven by the all-pervasive linguistic quality of dialect, from its typical sounds and phonotactics to syntax and from its pragmatics to its quality as a social, cultural and historical mirror. From 2016 on, that is, a 100 odd years after the publication of de Saussure's

Cours de linguistique générale, it seems high time for us to make sure that dialect, no matter whether we call it *système* or *parole*, is analysed systematically and computer-based. So let us, supported by *EDD Online*, start studying what could be called dialectal 'competence' without getting overwhelmed by the complexity of dialectal 'performance'.

Appendix

AFTER-DAMP, *sb.* Tech. Nhb. Dur. w.Yks. [**a·ftə-damp**.]
The noxious gas resulting from a colliery explosion
(Wedgwood).
Nhb. & Dur. After-damp, carbonic acid, stythe. The products
of the combustion of fire-damp, NICHOLSON *Coal Tr. Gl.* (1888)
Nhb.1 After-damp, the noxious gas resulting from a colliery explosion.
This after-damp is called choak-damp and surfeit by the
colliers, and is the carbonic acid gas of chymists, HODGSON *A
Description of Felling Colliery.* **w.Yks.** The after-damp completed
their death, *N. & Q.* (1876) 5th S. v. 325. Miners' tech. Carbonic
acid gas, or choke damp, which the miners call after-damp, Core
(1886) 228.
[*After + damp*, q.v.; cp. **choak-damp**.]

Figure 3.1 Main tags and layout in *EDD Online* (example AFTER-DAMP)

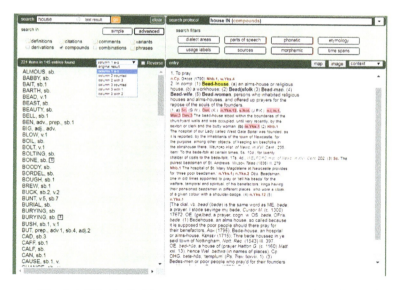

Figure 6.4 Identical with search in Figure 6.3, but with headwords sorted A–Z

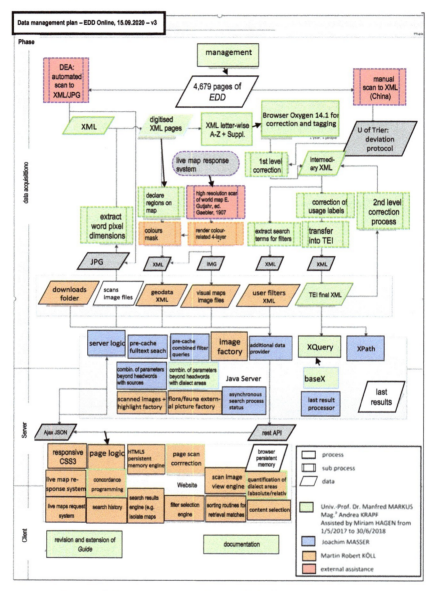

Figure 5.4 Data management plan of *EDD Online*

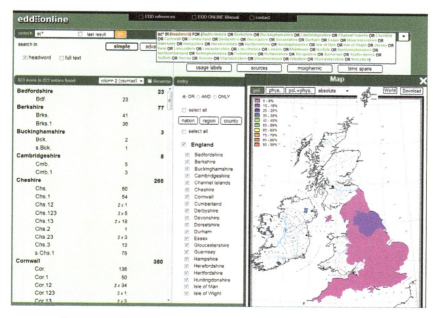

Figure 6.14 Distribution of *sc**-words in England (absolute figures)

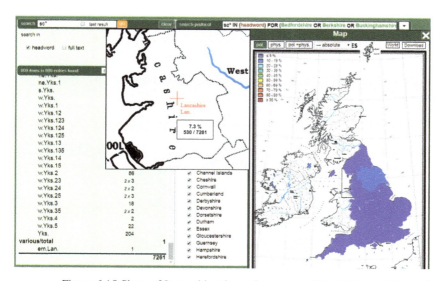

Figure 6.15 Share of Lancashire shown in pop-up window (in percentage of
the number of all English counties)

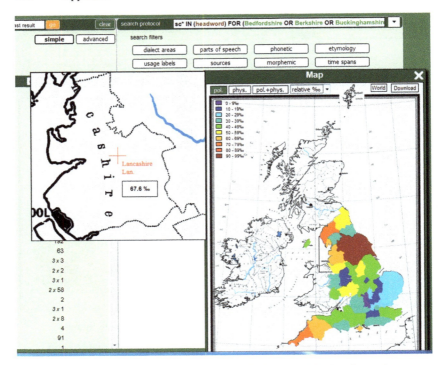

Figure 6.16 Distribution of *sc**-words in England (relative figures in *per thousand*), with a zoom on Lancashire

Figure 6.22 Search for χ (velar fricative) in *full text*

Figure 6.23 Search for [χ] (velar fricative) as a symbol of *phonetic transcription* in the filter option *full text* (right half of interface)

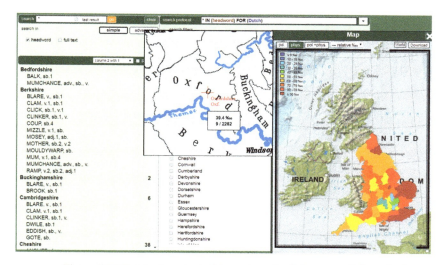

Figure 6.26 Dutch etymological impact on English county dialects (*column 2 with 1*)

Figure 7.3 Marking acceptable and unacceptable combinations of parameters and filters

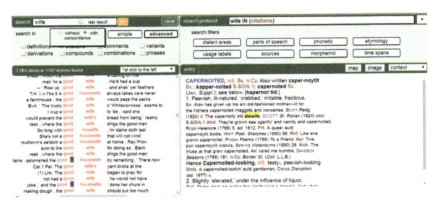

Figure 7.8 Kwik concordance of *wife* as keyword in the *citations* parameter, with left-side collocates (first slot)

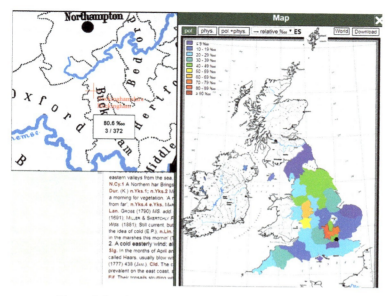

Figure 8.5 *H*-dropping (for <ha->): distribution illustrated on a map of the British Isles (relative per 10,000)

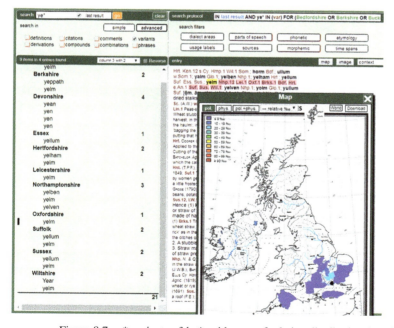

Figure 8.7 *ye**-variants of *ha**, with map of relative distribution (per 10,000)

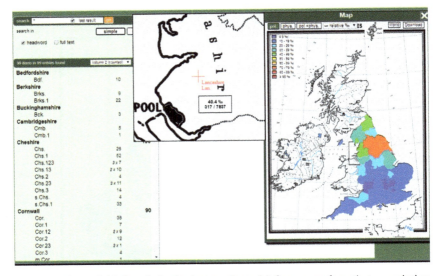

Figure 8.11 Search (in the last result mode) for χ as a *phonetic transcription* in *full text*, with a mapping of the English counties concerned (quantification in *per thousand*)

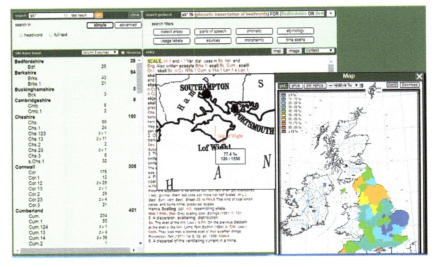

Figure 8.15 Map of relative figures concerning the headwords with *sk**-transcription county-wise

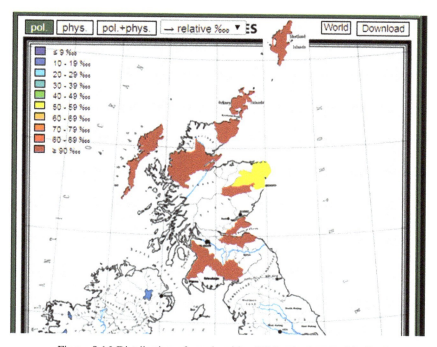

Figure 8.16 Distribution of words with a Viking background in Scotland

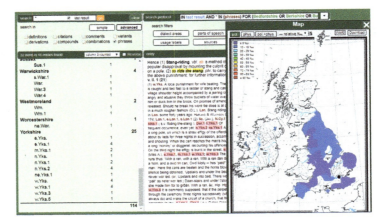

Figure 8.21 Rearrangement of the results of Figure 8.20 for phrases according to the dialectal areas concerned (after a last-result search)

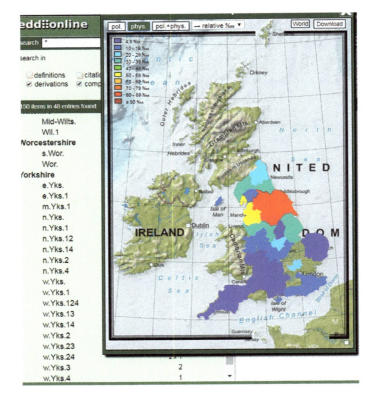

Figure 8.22 Map (per 10,000) illustrating the distribution of 339 derivations, compounds and combinations with *Gawain* background

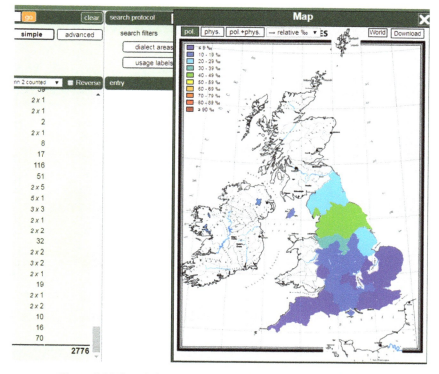

Figure 8.23 Search for monemes with *Gawain*-background plus map (per *thousand*)

Figure 8.25 Result of search for *orchis* in flora: 114 plant names

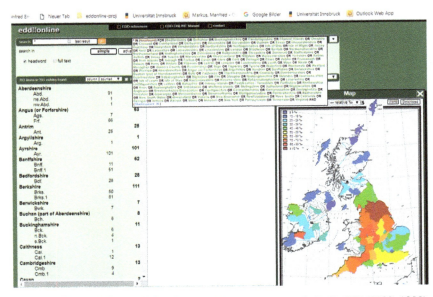

Figure 8.30 Areal distribution of Shakespeare words in the UK (1700–1900)

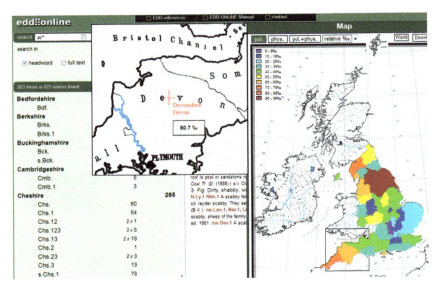

Figure 9.10 'Relative' mapping of all *sc**-words in England, quantified *per thousand*

References

Barnes, W. (1886). *A Glossary of the Dorset Dialect with a Grammar of Its Word Shapening and Wording*. London: Trübner and Co. (Repr. Stevens-Cox 1970.)

Beal, J. C. (2010). The Contribution of the Rev. Joseph Hunter's Hallamshire Glossary (1829) to Wright's *English Dialect Dictionary*. In M. Markus, C. Upton and R. Heuberger, eds., *Joseph Wright's English Dialect Dictionary and Beyond*. Studies in Late Modern English Dialectology. Frankfurt am Main: Peter Lang, pp. 39–48.

Bense, J. F. (1924). *The Anglo-Dutch Relations from the Earliest Times to the Death of William the Third [i.e. 1702], Being an Historical Introduction to a Dictionary of the Low-Dutch Element in the English Vocabulary*. Dordrecht: Springer Science + Business Media.

Benson, L. D. (1965). The Authorship of St. Erkenwald. *JEGP*, 64: 393–405.

Braber, N. and J. Robinson (2018). *East Midland English*. Dialects of English [DSOE] 15. New York: De Gruyter.

Brinton, L. J. and M. Akimoto, eds. (1999). *Collocational and Idiomatic Aspects of Composite Predicates in the History of English*. Studies in Language Companion Series 47. Amsterdam: Benjamins. (Review by Manfred Markus in *Anglia* 122 (2004), 491–4.)

Carver, C. M. (1989). *American Regional Dialects: A Word Geography*. Chicago: University of Michigan Press.

Cesiri, D. (2010). The 'Excluded Material' in Joseph Wright's *English Dialect Dictionary*. In M. Manfred, C. Upton and R. Heuberger, eds., *Joseph Wright's English Dialect Dictionary and Beyond*. Studies in Late Modern English Dialectology. Frankfurt am Main: Peter Lang, pp. 49–60.

Chamson, E. (2010). *The Continental West Germanic Heritage in Late Modern English Dialects. An Etymological Investigation of the English Dialect Dictionary*. Dissertation (unpublished), University of Innsbruck.

Chamson, E. (2012). Etymology in the English Dialect Dictionary. In M. Markus, Y. Iyeiri, R. Heuberger and E. Chamson, eds., *Middle and Modern English Corpus Linguistics: A Multi-dimensional Approach*. Amsterdam and Philadelphia: John Benjamins, pp. 225–40.

Davis, N., ed. (1968). *Sir Gawain and the Green Knight*. Edited by J. R. R. Tolkien and E. V. Gordon, Oxford: At the Clarendon Press, 2nd ed.

EDD Online 2.0. http://eddonline-proj.uibk.ac.at (= Innsbruck interface of the digitised *English Dialect Dictionary*), edited by M. Markus (2017) (accessed January 2018).

EDD Online 3.0. https://eddonline-proj.uibk.ac.at (= Innsbruck interface of the digitised *English Dialect Dictionary*), edited by M. Markus (2019) (accessed October 2019).

Ernst, P. (2008). *Dialektgeographie der Zukunft. Akten des 2. Kongresses der Internationalen Gesellschaft für Dialektologie des Deutschen (IGDD) am Institut für Germanistik der Universität Wien, 20. bis 23. September 2006.* Internationale Gesellschaft für Dialektologie des Deutschen. Stuttgart: Steiner.

Falkus, M. and J. Gillingham, eds. (1981). *Historical Atlas of Britain.* London: Granada.

Francis, W. N. (1983). *Dialectology. An Introduction.* London and New York: Longman.

Goebl, H. (1982). *Dialektometrie. Prinzipien und Methoden der Numerischen Taxometrie im Bereich der Dialektgeographie.* Vienna: Verlag der österreichischen Akademie der Wissenschaften.

Goebl, H. (2007). A Bunch of Dialect Metric Flowers: A Brief Introduction to Dialectometry. In U. Smit, S. Dollinger, J. Hüttner, G. Kaltenböck and U. Lutzky, eds., *Tracing English through Time: Explorations in Language Variation. In Honour of Herbert Schendl on the Occasion of His 65th Birthday.* Vienna: Braumüller, pp. 133–83.

Gollancz, Sir I., ed. (1940). *Sir Gawain and the Green Knight:* Re-edited from MS. *Cotton Nero A.x., in the British Museum. EETS OS 210.* London: Oxford University Press.

Grandage, S. (2016). Idioms, Proverbs, Quotations: Shakespeare's Influence on Language Evolution. In B. R. Smith (ed. and preface) and K. Rowe, eds., *The Cambridge Guide to the Worlds of Shakespeare.* New York: Cambridge University Press, pp. 1380–7.

Gries, S. T. (2015). Quantitative Designs and Statistical Techniques. In D. Biber and R. Reppen, eds., *The Cambridge Handbook of English Corpus Linguistics.* Cambridge: Cambridge University Press, pp. 50–71.

Grimm, J. and W. Grimm (2017). *Deutsches Wörterbuch* (digital): http://dwb.uni-trier .de/de/ (2 August 2017).

Harold, E. R. and W. Scott Means (2004). *XML in a Nutshell,* 3rd ed. Beijing and Cambridge: O'Reilly.

Herben, S. J. (1963). A Shakespearean Limerick. *Shakespeare Quarterly* 14: 481.

Howard, D. R. and C. Zacher, eds. (1968). *Critical Studies of* Sir Gawain and the Green Knight. Notre Dame, IN: University of Notre Dame Press.

Hughes, A., P. Trudgill and D. Watt (2005). *English Accents and Dialects: An Introduction to Social and Regional Varieties of English in the British Isles,* 4th ed. London: Hodder Arnold.

Illustrated Letters of the Paston Family (1989). Edited by R. Virgoe. New York: Weidenfeld and Nicolson.

Jamieson, J. (1808). *Etymological Dictionary of the Scottish Language,* 2 vols., Edinburgh. (New ed., carefully revised and collated, with the entire Supplement incorporated, by John Longmuir and David Donaldson, 4 vols., Paisley, 1879–82.)

Kaiser, R. (1937). *Zur Geographie des mittelenglischen Wortschatzes.* Leipzig: Mayer and Müller. (Repr. London/New York: Johnson 1970.)

Karl vom Ebbe (pseud. for Fritz Sträter) (2007). *Heiteres und Nachdenkliches über große & vor allem kleine Begebenheiten in & um Meinerzhagen – op Platt verfasst von Fritz Sträter.* Edited by D. Sträter, D. Sträter-Müller and U. Sträter. Meinerzhagen: Selbstverlag, www.karl-vom-ebbe.de/suche?id=17&keywords= besmen (accessed 24 March 2019).

Kastovsky, Dieter. 1968. *Old English Deverbal Substantives Derived By Means of a Zero Morpheme.* Esslingen: B. Langer.

Kolb, E., B. Glauser, W. Elmer and R. Stamm (1979). *Atlas of English Sounds.* Bern: Francke.

Kortmann, B. (2008). Synopsis: Morphological and Syntactic Variation in the British Isles. In B. Kortmann and C. Upton, eds., *Varieties of English. The British Isles.* Berlin and New York: Mouton de Gruyter, pp. 478–95.

Kortmann, B., T. Hermann, L. Pietsch and S. Wagner, eds. (2005). *A Comparative Grammar of British English Dialects: Agreement, Gender, Relative Clauses.* Berlin and New York: Mouton de Gruyter.

Legman, G. (1970). *The Limerick.* New York: Brandywine Press.

Leisi, E. and C. Mair (1953). *Das heutige Englisch. Wesenszüge und Probleme.* Heidelberg: C. Winter. (8th ed., 1999.)

Lutz, A. (1991). *Phonotaktisch gesteuerte Konsonantenveränderungen in der Geschichte des Englischen.* Tübingen: Max Niemeyer Verlag.

Madden, Sir F., ed. (1839). *Syr Gawayne; A Collection of Ancient Romance-Poems, by Scotish and English Authors, Relating to That Celebrated Knight of the Round Table,* with an Introduction, Notes, and a Glossary. London: Taylor.

Markus, M. (1971). *Moderne Erzählperspektive in den Werken des Gawain-Autors.* Regensburg and Nürnberg: Franz Karl Verlag.

Markus, M. (2002). The Genesis of H-Dropping Revisited: An Empirical Analysis. In K. Lenz and R. Möhlig, eds., *Of Dyuersitie and Chaunge of Language: Essays Presented to M. Görlach on the Occasion of His 65th Birthday.* Heidelberg: C. Winter, pp. 6–26.

Markus, M. (2010a). *As drunk as muck.* The Role and Logic of Similes in English Dialects on the Basis of Joseph Wright's *English Dialect Dictionary. Studia Philologica* 82: 203–16.

Markus, M. (2010b). Diminutives in English Standard and Dialects: A Survey Based on Wright's *English Dialect Dictionary.* In M. Markus, C. Upton and R. Heuberger, eds., *Joseph Wright's English Dialect Dictionary and Beyond: Studies in Late Modern English Dialectology.* Frankfurt am Main: Peter Lang, pp. 111–29.

Markus, M. (2011). *A Glass of Yale:* J-Insertion in English Dialects (Based on Joseph Wright's *English Dialect Dictionary).* In R. Bauer and U. Krischke, eds., *More than Words. English Lexicography and Lexicology Past and Present. Essays Presented to Hans Sauer on the Occasion of His 65th Birthday* – Part 1. Berlin: Peter Lang, pp. 329–54.

Markus, M. (2012). The Complexity and Diversity of the Words in Wright's *English Dialect Dictionary.* In M. Markus, Y. Iyeiri, R. Heuberger and E. Chamson, eds., *Middle and Modern English Corpus Linguistics: A Multi-dimensional Approach.* Amsterdam: John Benjamins, pp. 209–24.

Markus, M. (2015). Spoken Features of Interjections in English Dialect (Based on Joseph Wright's *English Dialect Dictionary).* In I. Taavitsainen, M. Kytö, C. Claridge and J. Smith, eds., *Developments in English. Expanding Electronic Evidence.* Cambridge: Cambridge University Press, pp. 116–34.

Markus, M. (2017a). Flora in the English Dialect Dictionary Online. *Transactions of the Yorkshire Dialect Society,* 1–6.

Markus, M. (2017b). The Use of EDD Online 3.0 – a Short Guide. Revised 2019. http://eddonline-proj.uibk.ac.at (accessed 30 October 2020).

Markus, M. (2017c). The Survival of Shakespeare's Language in English Dialects (on the Basis of *EDD Online*), *English Studies* 98: 881–96. (Chapter 2 also published online 8 September 2017: www.tandfonline.com/doi/full/10.1080/0013838X.2017.1365558)

Markus, M. (2018). Review of Monika Wegmann. 2017. *Language in Space: The Cartographic Representation of Dialects.* Travaux de Linguistique et de Philologie. Strasbourg: Éditions de Linguistique et de Philologie. (Rev. in *Anglia* 136(3): 530–7.)

Markus, M. (2019a). EDD Online: What Is New in Its Latest Version 3.0. In Dialectologia et Geolinguistica. *Journal of the International Society for Dialectology and Geolinguistics* 27: 103–21.

Markus, M. (2019b). The Supplement to the *English Dialect Dictionary*: Its Structure and Value as Part of *EDD Online*. *International Journal of Lexicography*, 2018, 32(1): 58–67.

McMahon, A. M. S. (1994). *Understanding Language Change.* Cambridge: Cambridge University Press.

Morris, R., ed. (1864). *Early English Alliterative Poems in the West-Midland Dialect of the Fourteenth Century. EETS* OS 1. London: Oxford University Press.

Nerbonne, J. and W. A. Kretschmar, Jr. (2013). Dialectometry ++. *Literary and Linguistic Computing* 28(1): 2–12.

Onysko, A. (2010). Phrases, Combinations and Compounds in the English Dialect Dictionary as a Source of Conceptual Metaphors and Metonymies in Late Modern English dialects. In M. Markus, C. Upton and R. Heuberger, eds., *Joseph Wright's English Dialect Dictionary and Beyond. Studies in Late Modern English Dialectology.* Frankfurt am Main: Peter Lang, pp. 129–53.

Orton, H. and N. Wright (1974). *A Word Geography of England.* London: Seminar Press.

Parry, D. (1977 and 1979). *The Survey of Anglo-Welsh Dialects,* 2 vols. Swansea: University College.

Praxmarer, C. (2010a). Joseph Wright's EDD and the Geographical Distribution of Dialects: A Visual Approach. In M. Markus, C. Upton and R. Heuberger, eds., *Joseph Wright's English Dialect Dictionary and beyond. Studies in Late Modern English Dialectology.* Frankfurt am Main: Peter Lang, pp. 61–73.

Praxmarer, C. (2010b). Dialect Relations in the English Dialect Dictionary. In *Proceedings of Methods XIII. Papers from the Thirteenth International Conference on Methods in Dialectology,* 2008. Frankfurt am Main: Peter Lang, pp. 153–9.

Rayson, P. (2015). Computational Tools and Methods for Corpus Compilation and Analysis. In *The Cambridge Handbook of English Corpus Linguistics.* Cambridge: Cambridge University Press, pp. 32–49.

Schälkle, K. and W. Ott (2015). *TUSTEP: Tübinger System von Textverarbeitungs-Programmen - Version 2016 : Handbuch und Referenz. Parametergesteuerte Programme, Programme und Makros zur Satzherstellung,* Register, Teil 2. Tübingen: pagina GmbH Publikationstechnologien.

Spearing, A. C. (1976). *Medieval Dream-Poetry.* Cambridge: Cambridge University Press.

Speitel, H. H. and J. Y. Mather, eds. (2010). *The Linguistic Atlas of Scotland*, 3 vols. London: Routledge.

Stratmann, F. H. (1891). *MED (A Middle-English Dictionary)*, New Edition by H. Bradley. Oxford: University Press. (Repr. 1967.)

Szmrecsanyi, B. (2013). *Grammatical Variation in British English Dialects. A Study in Corpus-Based Dialectometry*. Cambridge: Cambridge University Press.

Upton, C. and J. D. A. Widdowson (2006). *An Atlas of English Dialects*, 2nd ed. London: Routledge. (1st ed., 1996.)

Vennemann, T. (1988). *Preference Laws for Syllable Structure and the Explanation of Sound Change*. Berlin: Mouton de Gruyter.

Viereck, W. and H. Ramisch, eds. (1991–1997). *The Computer Developed Linguistic Atlas of England*, vol. 2. Tübingen: Niemeyer.

Viereck, K., W. Viereck and H. Ramisch (W. Wildermuth, illustrator) (2002). *dtv-Atlas Englische Sprache*. Munich: Dtv Verlagsgesellschaft.

Walmsley, P. (2007). *XQuery*. Beijing and Cambridge: O'Reilly.

Wegmann, M. (2016). *Language in Space: The Cartographic Representation of Dialects*. Strasbourg: Éditions de linguistique et de philologie.

Wright, E. M. (1932). *The Life of Joseph Wright*, 2 vols. London: Oxford University Press.

Wright, J. (1898–1905). *The English Dialect Dictionary*, 6 vols. Oxford: Henry Frowde.

Index